Love
and
Kisses
Jan :)

**100 food portraits
25 locations
4 seasons**

paul
cunningham

Copenhagen
Paris

food

Grub Street // London

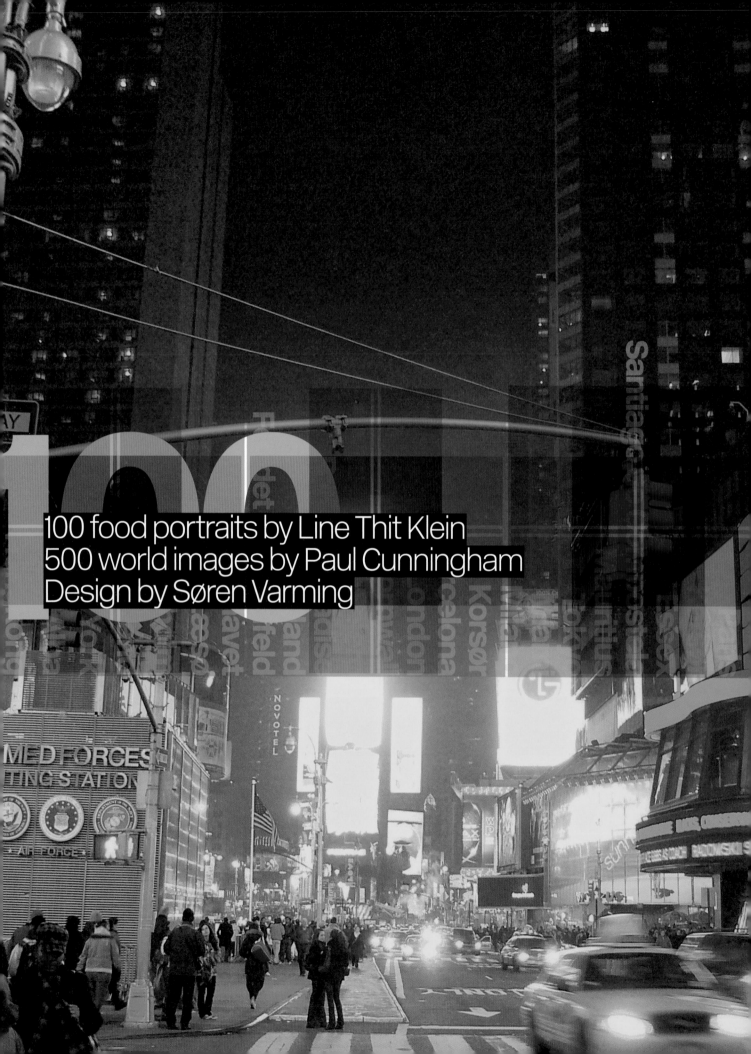

100 food portraits by Line Thit Klein
500 world images by Paul Cunningham
Design by Søren Varming

Santiago de compostela

Paris

Essex

This book is a gastronomic journey filled with food, places and people. *Paul Food* is a book of moments, my moments – and these moments, these destinations have meant a great deal to me.

The places have really moved me, the people I have come to love. From the flaming passion in Barcelona's old alleyways to the well anchored family values in the wild Basque mountains. Tokyo's streets full of honour, pride and history and Hong Kong's neon lit scenery, like a shot from Blade Runner, still haunt my dreams.

I fly to Sydney in a few days, and then onto old Shanghai. Vancouver, Palm Beach and New York beckon too – another volume is writing itself. Until then I do hope that you'll enjoy my moments within *Paul Food*.

Paul
Copenhagen, October 2012

Bits & pieces

When seasoning a dish always use **FRESHLY GROUND BLACK PEPPER** and **SEA SALT**.

Olive oil is always **COLD PRESSED EXTRA VIRGIN OLIVE OIL**.

The butter is always **SALTED**.

DAIRY PRODUCTS always come from **SMALL ORGANIC DAIRY FARMS**, where the focus is on taste.

Sugar is **UNREFINED LIGHT ORGANIC CANE SUGAR**.

A **SUGAR THERMOMETER** is not particularly expensive and can be a good investment.

STOCKS are always home made. You can find recipes for stock in most cookbooks – but not in this one. Alternatively you might be able to buy a small pot of stock from your local restaurant.

When using **EGGS**, always use **LARGE ORGANIC EGGS**.

When using **CHOCOLATE** in a recipe, use the best you can get hold of. I swear by **SCHARFFEN BERGER** or **VALRHONA** of around the 70% cacao mark.

I always use **TAHITI** or **TONGA VANILLA**, but Bourbon vanilla is also superb. Infuse the empty vanilla pods in a glass jar with cane sugar. You'll have vanilla'ed sugar, whenever you need it.

When using **FRESH CHILLI** I usually remove the seeds.

MAYONNAISE – make it yourself or use Hellmànn's mixed with a drop of olive oil.

When bread or toast is called for I use a good **SOURDOUGH**.

Buy good quality **PUFF PASTRY** made from butter and not margarine. Otherwise you can make it yourself, it freezes most delightfully.

SALAD DRESSING: 1 tsp Dijon mustard, ½ tsp sugar, 100 ml Sherry vinegar, 300 ml olive oil, salt and pepper.

VENTRÈCHE is air dried pepper bacon from the south west of France. If you cannot get hold of it or are unable to buy it from your local restaurant then use dry smoked bacon or Italian pancetta instead.

PANKO are Japanese breadcrumbs which you can buy from Asian grocers.

Invest in some decent **KNIVES**. A small vegetable knife, a filleting knife and a large kitchen knife. Mac, Global, Sabatier are superb, handmade Japanese knives are pure works of art.

Use disposable **LATEX** or **PLASTIC GLOVES**, when working with smoked fish or other smoked food, and you won't smell like an old dock worker when your guests arrive.

Buy a **MICRO PLANE GRATER** for grating and a **JAPANESE MANDOLINE** for slicing finely, both are just the thing.

With a couple of **NON-STICK** pans and maybe a large enamelled **LE CREUSET** cast iron saucepan you will be well off – buy the orange one of course!

If you are making **SORBET** without an ice machine, pour it into a bowl, place in the freezer and stir it every 15 minutes, until the sorbet has set.

It's not maybe necessary to remind you that you should only use **FRESH INGREDIENTS**.

ACCOMPANIMENTS and **SIDES** to go with the individual dishes, you may choose yourself.

When I talk about **RESTING TIME** in food preparation, I generally refer to the dish, and not the cook. It simply means that the dish needs to rest a little before it is cut, served and enjoyed.

ORANGES, LEMONS and **LIMES** are always organic, and unsprayed, especially when using the zest.

Winter

Copenhagen

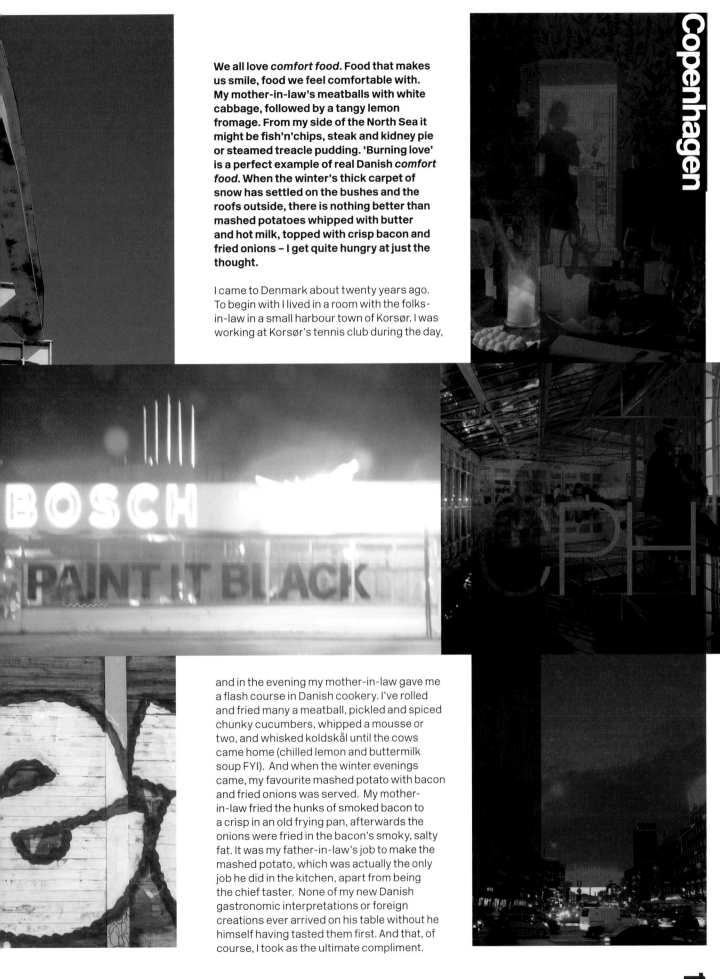

We all love *comfort food*. Food that makes us smile, food we feel comfortable with. My mother-in-law's meatballs with white cabbage, followed by a tangy lemon fromage. From my side of the North Sea it might be fish'n'chips, steak and kidney pie or steamed treacle pudding. 'Burning love' is a perfect example of real Danish *comfort food*. When the winter's thick carpet of snow has settled on the bushes and the roofs outside, there is nothing better than mashed potatoes whipped with butter and hot milk, topped with crisp bacon and fried onions – I get quite hungry at just the thought.

I came to Denmark about twenty years ago. To begin with I lived in a room with the folks-in-law in a small harbour town of Korsør. I was working at Korsør's tennis club during the day,

and in the evening my mother-in-law gave me a flash course in Danish cookery. I've rolled and fried many a meatball, pickled and spiced chunky cucumbers, whipped a mousse or two, and whisked koldskål until the cows came home (chilled lemon and buttermilk soup FYI). And when the winter evenings came, my favourite mashed potato with bacon and fried onions was served. My mother-in-law fried the hunks of smoked bacon to a crisp in an old frying pan, afterwards the onions were fried in the bacon's smoky, salty fat. It was my father-in-law's job to make the mashed potato, which was actually the only job he did in the kitchen, apart from being the chief taster. None of my new Danish gastronomic interpretations or foreign creations ever arrived on his table without he himself having tasted them first. And that, of course, I took as the ultimate compliment.

This dish is for me *comfort food deluxe*. The Paul had 'burning love' on the menu for many years, served in as many different versions. Our *pommes mousselines* are equal parts potatoes and butter with a little hot milk. Healthy it is not, but heavenly it is. Instead of bacon we have often used crisp salty pork crackling, while the fried onions have been replaced by fresh, sharp spring onions. Roasted Danish lobster or Læsø langoustines sprinkled with freshly cut chives work magically. Here I've used caviar as the sharp, salty element in the dish. The mashed potato or *pommes mousselines* is flavoured with chopped shallots and a little dice of cold smoked beef bone marrow – which might be a little difficult to find, but do try to ask your friendly butcher if he can get hold of half a kilo for you. It keeps well in the freezer. The boned marrow is salted for a while in brine and then cold smoked transforming it into something quite unique.

FOR FOUR

I bake four thick fillets of cod, approx. 100g per head in the oven for 10 minutes at 180°C/gas 4 with butter and a little sea salt. Leave the cod to rest while you mash the boiled potatoes with the same amount of butter and a teaspoon of chopped smoked beef marrow per person and a finely chopped shallot. Season the potato with a little sea salt and a tiny squeeze of lemon. Do not heat the *pommes mousselines* too much after this point, it'll split if boiled!

Arrange the cod on top of the potato topped with caviar and a couple of extra slices of warmed smoked beef marrow. Remember the cooking juices from the fish and a little lemon juice. Sprinkle with salt crystals.

Comfort food my way – should be eaten with a spoon and with those you love.

Potato puree, baked cod, caviar & smoked beef marrow

001

Breakfast at Big Ben's

002

In England we love our big breakfasts, maybe not every day, but now and then we need to *go for it* – and we *went for it* at Ben's place that day. It was little Ben's birthday and all was perfect. The only missing thing was *a jar of Marmite*!

FOR THREE BRITS AND A YANK

Brush eight small Italian fennel sausages with a little olive oil and bake for 15 minutes in a hot oven, 180°C/gas 4. Remove from the oven and keep warm.

Fry to a crisp four thick slices of English black pudding or French *boudin noir*. (Danish black pudding is just too sweet, usually eaten at Christmas time with brown sugar and cinnamon.)

Roast four thick slices of foie gras, approx. 100 g per slice. Golden brown, one to two minutes on each side. Season with sea salt and freshly ground black pepper.

Soft poach four eggs in a large saucepan with boiling water, salted with a touch of vinegar.

Serve with toast – or better still, toasted brioche and plenty of milky Earl Grey.

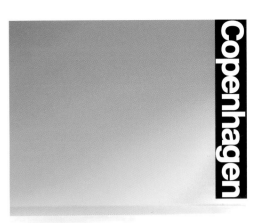

Chicken'n'caviar

003

A crisp decadent winter snack, dedicated to my best friend Hans V and his most lovely Maria, of the equally decadent Chez Dominique in Helsinki.
It is salty and rich. It's vulgar – positively meant of course. As an appetiser with a glass of Champagne or with a gin and tonic, but has also adorned my twisted version of Salade Caesar Cardini more than once, at The Paul.

A strange command but save all of your chicken skin when making stocks, soups or poaching for salads (skin and fat are a homemade stock's worst enemy, resulting in a cloudy, fatty bouillon). Scrape the skin with the blunt side of a knife. Place the thin pieces of chicken skin between two pieces of baking paper and freeze them for when you have guests next time.

Warm your oven to 170°C/gas 3½. Take the skin out of the freezer and sprinkle it with fine sea salt. Bake the salted skin for about 45 minutes golden and crisp between two silicone mats under a little pressure (baking paper works fine too). Serve the crisp salty chicken skin warm, topped with caviar, trout roe or lightly salted lumpfish roe.

Every good meal starts with two very simple, but crucial elements – good bread and good butter. There is nothing like the taste, and feeling of warm freshly baked bread with lovely cold salted butter, made with love by a dedicated dairy.

Manitoba cream is a particular type of Canadian wheat flour with very high gluten content. It makes a most elastic dough and a bread of intense flavour, crisp crust and soft centre not unlike my beloved English crumpets.

FOR 30 SMALL BUNS OR TWO LARGER LOAVES

30 g fine sea salt
15 g sugar
20 g fresh yeast
750 ml warm water
700 g Manitoba flour
150 g malt flour

DAY 1
Dissolve the salt, sugar and yeast in the warm water. Set aside for 10 minutes. Add both types of flour and mix the dough in the food mixer for 10-12 minutes at high speed. Pour the dough into a container brushed with oil and leave to cool overnight.

DAY 2
Warm your oven to 200°C/gas 6. The dough is rather soft, so you will need to lift the dough and clip it out of the container with lightly oiled scissors, we place the small doughs directly into small oiled silicone muffin moulds or bread tins.

Leave for approx. one and a half hours in a warm place before baking. The buns will take about 25 minutes and the loaves around 45. Oven temperatures vary so if in doubt, take the bread out of the oven and carefully remove it from the tin – if it feels light and sounds hollow when tapped it's ready.

Leave to rest and enjoy with lashings of brilliant butter.

Malted Manitoba & our beautiful butter

004

West coast
turbot, Jerusalem
artichokes & caviar

005

My good friend Erik gave me boxes of these ancient plates. Hand painted Bing and Grøndahl from the end of the 1940's, before Royal Copenhagen was Royal Copenhagen. Produced under commission for the restaurant 'Damhuskroen', a Copenhagen institution for laughter and dancing girls since 1682!

FOR FOUR COSY DANES
4 large Jerusalem artichokes, peeled and rubbed with a little lemon juice
1 extra slice of lemon
Butter
100 ml of rich chicken stock made from the carcasses of a few roasted chickens
4 super fresh turbot fillets, each about 120 g
Olive oil
Caviar
Spanish chervil (Myrrhis odorata)
Sea salt and pepper

Poach the Jerusalem artichokes, al dente in well salted water with a slice of lemon. Pour off the water and glaze them with a little butter. Season.

Reduce the chicken stock, season with salt and pepper and lemon juice. Whisk in a good large spoonful of cold butter. Fry the turbot fillets golden in a little olive oil and a knob of butter. Season well with sea salt and fresh pepper.

Serve the glorious fish with the buttered Jerusalem artichokes, caviar, chervil and sauce.

Mmm...

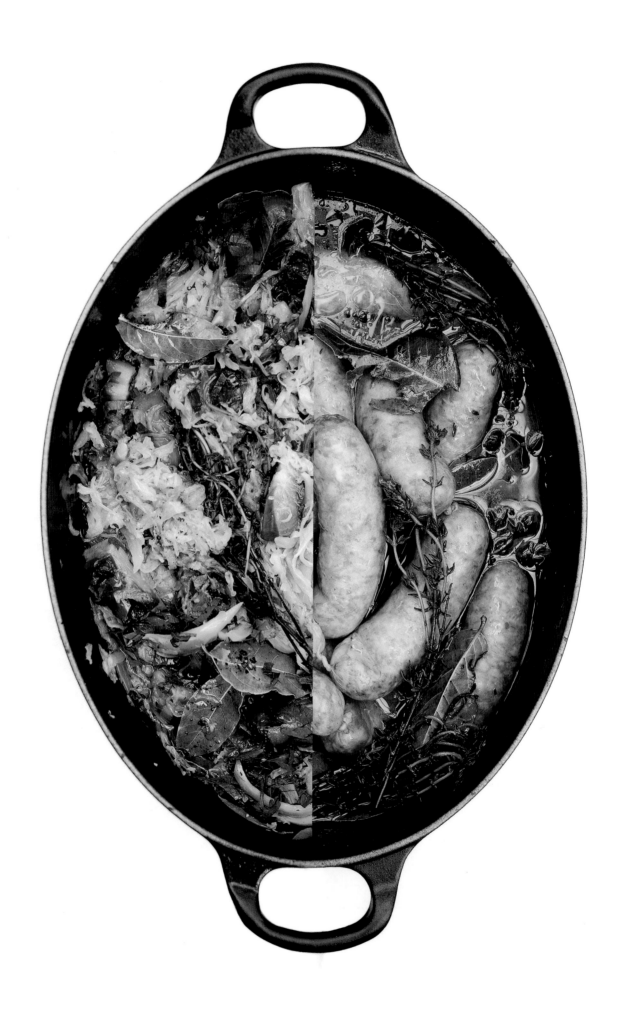

Sauerkraut, surkål, choucroute, pickled cabbage... the sour child has many names! This is my bid for one of Germany's most important national dishes, as I served it during the last German held World Cup. If you, as I did, forget to make the pickled the cabbage three weeks before, then do as 82 million other Germans do – buy it in a tin...

FOR TWO SWEATY SOUTHERN JUTLAND HOOLIGANS, ONE GERMAN AND A BRIT

STEP 1 – if you are well prepared
1 super-finely sliced white cabbage
12 juniper berries, crushed
150 g sea salt

Mix the cabbage well with juniper berries and salt. In a plastic container, under a weight, put in a refrigerator, cool larder or cellar for three weeks.

STEP 2
300 g superbly strong smoked bacon, cut into large cubes
4 onions, sliced
50 ml duck fat
2 large sprigs of thyme
6 bay leaves

Brown the bacon and onions in a large frying pan in the duck fat.

Wash the cabbage thoroughly in lots of fresh cold water, drain very well. You will need to squeeze really, really hard! Add the cabbage to the pan, together with the bacon and the onions, add the thyme and bay leaves. Braise the cabbage slowly over low heat for three hours. If you think it gets too dry then add a little water. Season the cabbage well with pepper but be careful with the salt! Spice up with a lashing of white wine or apple vinegar.

STEP 3
8, 12 or 16 handmade pork rich sausages from south Jutland
600 g finished pickled cabbage
A handful of chopped parsley
Ground black pepper
A little apple or white wine vinegar

Poach the sausages in water. Heat the cabbage thoroughly and mix it with chopped parsley, pepper and a little white wine vinegar. Put on Champions League and serve cabbage and sausages with cold beer and lots of strong mustard.

Soured cabbage with sausages from Southern Jutland

006

My mate Ben and I were January pale, and tired, when one Copenhagen winter's day, whilst peering out of the half-steamed window of our local coffee bar, we were struck by an overpowering light – the multicoloured Mecca that was our forgotten Thai supermarket on Istedgade, a colourful street and Denmark's answer to London's neon lit Soho streets. This recipe will bring a little colour into your drab winter but don't panic if you cannot get hold of all the vegetables and fruits. The dressing can be made in advance if you do not add the spring onion and it will keep for a while in the fridge.

FOR FOUR BIG SALADS

2 ripe Thai mangoes – ma muanq
2 papayas
1 large handful fresh ripe Jack fruit – kahnun/pitaya
1 large ripe white dragon fruit
2 small yellow dragon fruits
4 tamarillos
12 lychees
1 guava
12 okra – grajiab
4 baby aubergines – makeua
4 yellow aubergines
1 small handful small green aubergines – makeua puong
8 small red shallots – hom dang
12 spring onions – ton hwam
2 red chillies
2 yellow chillies
Fresh coriander – pak chee
Fresh mint
Sweet Thai basil – horapha

DRESSING
Seeds and juice from 2 passion fruits
Seeds and juice from 2 ripe pomegranates
1 tsp fresh green Madagascar peppercorns, crushed
½ tsp chopped green chilli
½ tsp chopped red chilli
2 cloves garlic, crushed
2 finely sliced spring onions
1 tsp fresh finely chopped galangal (kha) or ginger
1 tsp very finely chopped lemongrass
2 finely chopped kaffir lime leaves – bai ma kruut
4 tbsp Thai fish sauce – nam pla
1 tbsp palm sugar
4 tbsp soya light
4 tbsp toasted sesame oil
Juice and grated peel of an organic lime

Start with the dressing. Mix all the ingredients together and leave for a minimum of two hours. Wash, slice and chop all the fruits and vegetables as shown in the picture. Grill the vegetables. Place the ingredients in a large bowl and mix the salad and herbs thoroughly with the dressing.

ARO! MAK MAK!

Sweet, sour, salty & sunny Thai winter salad

007

It was Jan 'Cocotte' Pedersen who brought Babette's famous menu to life on the screen in the filming of Babette's Feast. Jan Pedersen was also the first Danish chef to receive a Michelin star with his restaurant La Cocotte in 1982. Jan is my friend and I had the honour of working with him for a couple of years at the end of the nineties when I first arrived at Søllerød Kro. Babette's menu started with blinis Demidoff and mock turtle soup. Truffled Cailles en Sarcophage followed, cheese and finally baba au rhum. Jan has been my mentor, big love my Lord.

FOR FOUR

4 boned quails (chat with your friendly butcher boy)
Fresh truffle
4 pieces of fresh foie gras at 50 g pp
4 large puff pastry vol-au-vents, 12 cm in diameter
a little melted butter

Place the whole boned quails on a chopping board. Sprinkle them inside with a touch of fine sea salt and a little freshly ground black pepper. Place a few slices of truffle in the middle of the breasts of each quail and then place a piece of fresh foie gras on top of the truffle. Season with a little more sea salt and pepper. Wrap the foie gras with the quail, creating the birds form once again, and place in the baked puff pastry coffins. Brush well with melted butter, sprinkle with a little sea salt and bake in a hot oven at 180°C/gas 4 for about 20 minutes.

Serve with a little buttered spinach and not much more – oh! don't forget the sauce.

SAUCE PERIGOURDINE
100 ml fino sherry
200 ml Madeira
200 ml strong poultry stock, made from the quails' roasted carcasses
1 little fresh truffle, finely chopped
40 g cold butter, cubed

Pour sherry and Madeira into a small warm saucepan. Reduce to about two tablespoons. Add the stock and leave the sauce to simmer and reduce a little with the chopped truffle.

Just before serving whisk the truffle sauce with the small cold butter cubes – *monter au beurre*, giving the sauce its fine sheen, a rich almost creamy flavour. The sauce must under no circumstances boil after this, otherwise it will split. Don't forget to season the sauce with a little sea salt and maybe a squeezette of lemon.

Bon appetit! Respect Jan P.

Cailles en Sarcophage.
Jan 'Cocotte' Pedersen

008

Tournedos is an ultra low-fat cut of beef, it needs fat and it needs salt. My logical, if a little different answer to this equation came when planning a caviar dinner for my pal and caviar-pusher Jacob Rossini.

FOR FOUR

4 small tournedos each 90 g, trimmed
4 cloves of garlic
4 fresh sprigs of thyme
2 sprigs of rosemary
4 slices of fresh foie gras each 50 g
4 sourdough bread croutons
1 fresh truffle
Olive oil
Butter
Sea salt and freshly ground black pepper
Ripe Baerii caviar

Brush the tournedos with olive oil and brown well in a good heavy cast iron pan. Add a generous tablespoon of butter, thyme, rosemary and garlic. Pan-roast the tournedos carefully while constantly basting with the, by now, well caramelized herb butter. It will take five minutes, the tournedos will be wonderfully rare inside. Season well with sea salt and freshly ground black pepper.

Let the tournedos rest whilst you pan-roast the foie gras, golden brown. This should be done carefully in a clean hot pan with a tiny film of olive oil. Roast for two-three minutes max, season well and place on top of the warm tournedos. Crisp the bread croutons in the foie gras render.

Place the tournedos on top of the foie-croutons with the foie, poised on top. Then sliced fresh truffle, finish with a rich Baerii caviar. A truffle sauce, pinched from the previous recipe would also be a nice addition.

… tournedos Rossini for Rossini.

Tournedos Rossini Rossini

009

Paris

CDG

This recipe is from the old chef at Fleur de Lys, a typical English country pub in the glorious village of Widdington, near Saffron Walden.

I was working at a cement factory in my hometown, when one day my sister's pal's father asked me if I would like to be a chef. He had been spying upon my creative gene, flicking through my drawings and photographs, suspecting that maybe my creativity could be used for something else than just doodling and snapping around at the weekends. He purchased the little pub in the most idyllic English village and threw me into the kitchen. Palates and plates became my new canvas, food and flavour my medium.

I spent a couple of weeks in the kitchen with the old chef David; he very kindly whipped me through the basics. His last night was a Sunday, and on the following Monday I would be there alone. After a sleepless night I rolled down the stairs in extra good time to make sure everything was ready. There was I, dressed in the tallest chef's hat my mum had been able to find, waiting for my first order, cup of tea in my trembling hand. At twelve o'clock the barman put his head through the kitchen and ordered two Truite amandine... the only dish on the entire menu that I had not seen David prepare, and which I hadn't the faintest idea how to create, my life was over!

FOR FOUR

4 sparklingly fresh rainbow trout, cleaned and trimmed
100 g melted butter
Sea salt and freshly ground black pepper
100 g flaked almonds
Lemon
Parsley, washed and chopped

Brush the fish well, both inside and out, with the melted butter and season with sea salt and fresh black pepper. Place the fish under a hot grill for four to five minutes on each side, depending on the size. Dress with the almonds and toast gently. Serve piping hot with fresh lemon juice, parsley and boiled new potatoes.

PS – I managed to get through the first day at Fleur de Lys... well I don't remember anybody returning any food and I definitely didn't kill anyone.

Truite amandine

010

9

A Parisian classic, mentioned in virtually all guides of this great city. During the 70's it was virtually impossible to visit a restaurant in the French capital without coming across this iconic, now almost retro dish. Indonesian long pepper peps up this dish with a slightly acidic bitter note, which suits the fatty duck most delightfully.

FOR FOUR

2 unsprayed Seville oranges if available
4 duckling breasts
Sea salt and Indonesian long pepper
A little olive oil
2 tbsp honey
50 g cold butter

Zest the oranges, peel them and cut out the segments, retaining all of the juices.

Season the duckling breasts well with sea salt and finely grated long pepper. Brush the breasts with a tiny film of olive oil and pan-roast slowly, skin side down, for 10 minutes, until the fat has rendered and the skin is golden and crisp. Turn the breasts and remove the pan from the heat, baste the breasts with the juices from the warm pan, the residual heat will finish the cooking process.

After resting the duckling, remove and plate, returning the pan to a high heat. Add the orange zest, juice and honey to the peppery duck juices. Reduce to a wonderful sticky consistency and whisk in the cold butter, throwing in the orange segments before serving over the golden duckling breasts – a touch more grated Indonesian long pepper gives that last touch of perfumed aroma.

Duck à l'orange

011

Bo and I were sitting at Chez l'Ami Louis, my favourite of Paris's numerous brasseries, and thoroughly *fantastique* it is too. While we were tucking into *foie gras de maison* with toasted brioche, huge scallops à la Provençale, *poularde de Bresse rotie* with fresh watercress, I spied upon another table, tiny *fraises des bois* with thick, heavy crème fraîche. *Parfait*. But before, during and after every good pudding, I cannot stop dreaming of their cheese. *Fromages français* is simply great and for me there is one in particular.

Epoisses is one of my absolute favourite cheeses. A great winter dinner is simply not right without this little, fat, round, rich, super creamy, superbly intense cheese from Burgundy. A cheese made from the freshest of cow's milk. Napoleon was said to have washed it down with his finest Chambertin. The quiet monks at Abbaye de Citeaux near the town Epoisses, first made this not-so-quiet cheese. Most complex with many tones, a strong cheese, but still also fine and soft on the palate and with a beautifully creamy structure. Lightly sweet and delightfully salty, the cheese is ripened in damp cellars for at least three months, and then washed several times in their very own marc de Bourgogne. During this maturing process the surface changes from ivory to dark deep orange.

Brillat-Savarin (who incidentally gave his name to his own fromage) rightly named Epoisses de Bourgogne, king of cheese. Produced by families in and around the town, it received AOC status in 1991. An attempt to mass-produce it some years ago, luckily failed.

By the way Stinking Bishop would be a great British substitute for Epoisses.

FOR FOUR *EPOISSEISTS*

1 small handful green seedless grapes
4 tbsp marc de Bourgogne
1 whole Epoisses de Bourgogne (should be at room temperature)
Fresh beautiful wild watercress

Leave the grapes to marinade in marc overnight. Preheat the oven to 180°C/gas 4.

Place the cheese in an ovenproof glass bowl, bake for eight minutes and serve with watercress and marc'ed grapes. Toasted wholemeal or rye too is lovely.

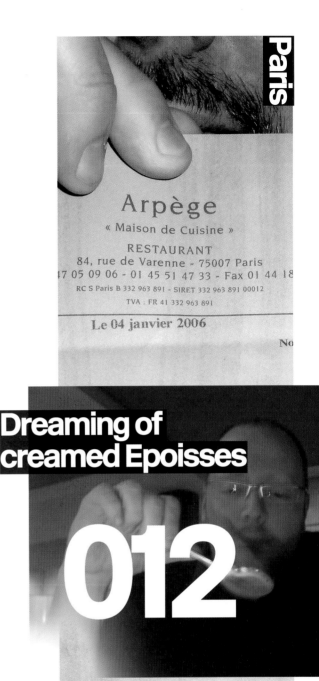

Dreaming of creamed Epoisses

012

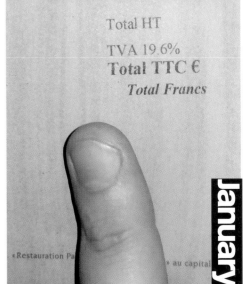

I once stayed in the legendary Hotel Costes in Paris. The former brothel is most well endowed in all that is dark purple, the furniture deep red velour and the black painted facade is quintessentially hip.

We ordered a little Champagne and studied the menu. I wanted everything, but my eyes were fixed upon Filet de tigre. Filet de tigre? A spelling mistake surely?

Our waitress looked like someone central casting had found for the job. Clever, knowledgeable enough I imagine she was, but really hot. She could have sold us anything.

'Eh....filet de tigre? 'I asked politely.

'Oui, monsieur,' she replied with the most shy and sweetest French school-girl accent.

I melted completely. We were certain it would turn out to be a very interesting evening.

It was too late now, no backing down, so boldly I ordered the tiger fillet, while wondering if I had indeed ordered a prime cut of meat from one of the globe's most threatened animals.

I must have looked most pale indeed when she returned with our orders... I felt a soft petite hand on my shoulder, and the sweet voice from earlier explaining that it was not a tiger grilled and lying dormant on my plate, but simply the cut of beef called *onglet* or hanger steak in English. Every proud bistro owner in France has onglet on the menu. It is also called *la pièce du boucher* since it tastes so good that the butcher keeps precisely that piece for himself. But Hotel Costes is after all a little more posh than the bistro round the corner, so they had decided to rename the peasant dish with something more exotic to say the least, and on top of that covered it in a sticky Thai sauce. But delicious it was. And Hotel Costes has after all this underground, exotic facade to keep up. I just wish I could afford to stay there every time I'm in town.

I brought the idea back to Copenhagen, gave the dish a twist and served it for the Queen. She loved it.

FOR FOUR

2 tomatoes
Olive oil
Mature beautiful thick balsamic vinegar
Salt and pepper
Sugar
4 onglets each 150 g, trimmed
4 red onions with top
Rocket, wild if you can get it when in season

Preheat the oven to 110°C/gas ¼. Cut the tomatoes in half and remove the seeds. Place on a baking tray lined with baking paper with the skin side down. Dress with olive oil and a few drops of balsamic vinegar, season with sea salt, pepper and a touch of sugar. Bake the tomatoes for six hours. Jar with the liquor and leave to infuse overnight.

Brush the *onglets* with a little olive oil, season with sea salt and fresh pepper, cover and place on one side for two hours. Grill on a very hot grill pan or over hot coals for half a minute on each side. They should have a dark charred crust, bordering on blackened and be red or rather *bleu* inside.

Leave the meat to rest for 10 minutes. In the meantime grill the onions that are cut into halves lengthwise, season and brush with olive oil. Serve the meat with the tomatoes and grilled onion, firey, peppered rocket leaves, a little extra brilliant olive oil, balsamic vinegar, sea salt and fresh pepper.

Filet de tigre?
Oui, monsieur!

013

Roasted foie gras is intense, rich, bombastic and decadently masculine. Now and then a fix of foie can be heavenly. It will need an accompaniment with plenty of acid to keep the fat levels in check. Green Puy lentils together with small vegetables, spiked well with lemon juice and red wine vinegar is a delicious, crisp, fresh and interesting salad that will cut the richness. Chilli will also cut through the liver's intensity. Roasted rhubarb goes real well, the same applies for pineapple, peach, green apples and even pomegranate seeds.

It was the ancient Egyptians who first explored the delights of foie gras back in the days around 2500BC. Today the best foie gras is often produced at small family-run farms in the south west of France and in Alsace. Delightful with a red Burgundy or prepared in a terrine and washed down with a sweeter fuller white wine from Alsace maybe. Personally I prefer the duck liver to somewhat richer, fattier goose liver.

FOR FOUR

200 g Puy lentils, rinsed well in lots of cold water
1 sprig of thyme
1 sprig of rosemary
4 bay leaves

2 cloves garlic, crushed
2 shallots, finely chopped
1 carrot, cut into small cubes
1 finely chopped red chilli, no seeds
1 small handful finely chopped broad leaved parsley
4 tomatoes – skinned, seeds removed, cut into fine cubes concassé
Zest and segments of 1 lemon
50 ml red wine vinegar
100 ml really good olive oil
Salt and freshly ground black pepper

1 fresh duck foie gras of approx. 400-500 g

Just cover the rinsed lentils with fresh cold water and simmer until tender, together with the thyme, rosemary and bay leaves. Stir through the other ingredients and season the salad well. Keep warm whilst you cook the foie gras.

Colour the foie gras in a hot pan until golden brown and caramelised. Season well with fine sea salt and freshly ground black pepper. Place into a hot oven set at 220°C/gas 7, and bake until the central temperature of the foie gras is at 55°C – using a cooking thermometer. Leave to rest for 10 minutes before serving.

Foie gras with Puy lentil salad

014

This little number is strongly inspired by Alain Passard from the three star L'Arpège on rue de Varenne within the seventh arrondissement in Paris. Probably the best and most definitely the most expensive meal I have ever embarked upon. Bo laughed so much when I studied the menu that he asked for the ladies menu for me – without prices!

Passard's speciality are dishes created from rare vegetables from his own gardens, a little shellfish, seldom fish and the odd bird or two occasionally land on his *carte du jour* – there's not a *steak frit* to be seen. On that particular night though, we were indeed presented with something so spectacularly simple it pushed me over the edge. Passard's *poulet* baked in hay was masterful – we were speechless.

We left euphorically that night. If only my wife was in sight – sons would have been conceived.

Guinea fowl Passard

015

MY OWN LITTLE HERBAL BAKED BIRD FOR FOUR

1 large fresh free range guinea fowl at around 2 kg
150 g melted butter
Sea salt and freshly ground pepper
1 large bouquet of fresh herbs, from the garden, if possible, for
   example tarragon, lovage, parsley, thyme, rosemary, sage,
   heather, lavender, basil, oregano, marjoram, mint – the more,
   the merrier

Brush the guinea fowl thoroughly, both inside and out with the melted butter and season well. Rinse the herbs and stuff one third of them inside the guinea fowl. Secure with string.

Place the guinea fowl in a deep casserole with a further third of the fresh herbs. Place a lid on the pot and roast the bird at 175°C/gas 4 for approx. 1½ hours, basting the guinea fowl from time to time. Remove the pan from the oven, remove the herbs and replace with the remaining third of the fresh herbs. Quickly replace the lid and leave to rest for 15 minutes, leaving the bird to herb-infuse once again.

Put the casserole directly on the table but without having lifted the lid. Only to be opened at the table, the air will be perfumed with the aromas of the herb-roasted bird. Carve and serve the guinea fowl with the buttered juices from the pot, together with a few simple vegetables and boiled potatoes, or indeed just a few dressed salad leaves and a good bread.

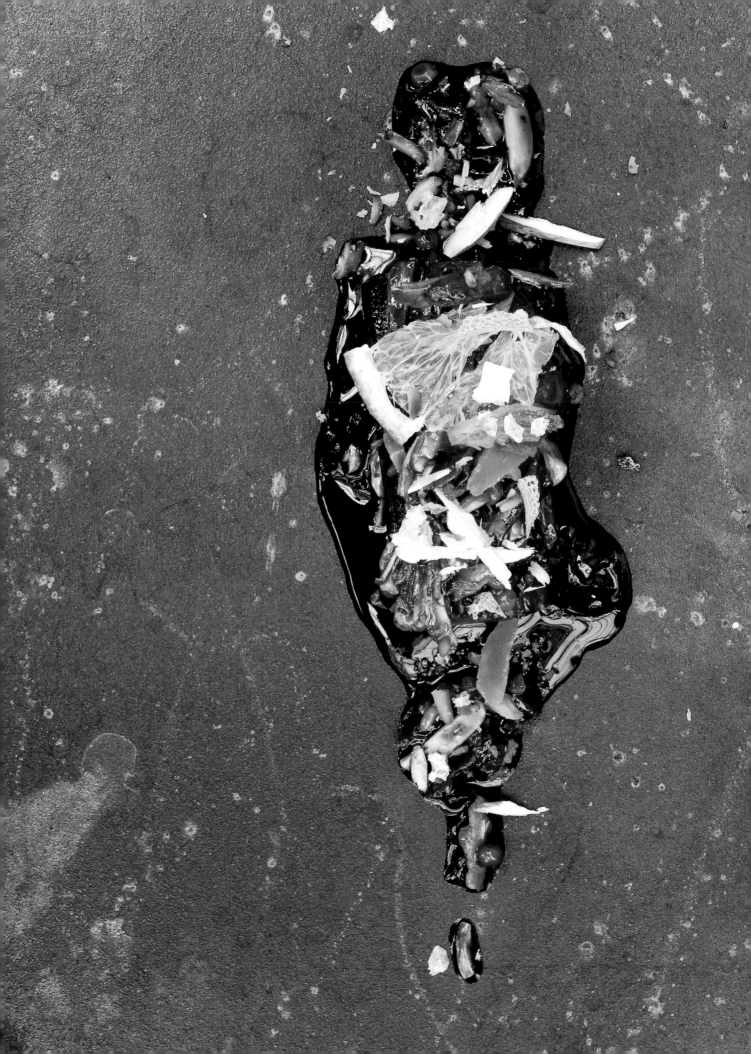

The sauce is every chef's secret. *Jus*, as we call it. The rich, dark, intensely sticky affair which sticks to the roof of your mouth and leaves you longing for more. This savoury umami experience will stay with you all evening. Your dinner party will never be the same again once you have excelled with such a sauce.

Real sauce takes time, care and patience. Get up early, and since a real sauce cannot be made without a really good stock, there is no time to lose.

This is my recipe for our venison sauce, enriched with dark chocolate, dried fruit and roasted nuts. If it is for roast prime rib of beef or a grilled tournedos, the venison bones are replaced with just the bones of beef or veal, and if the menu is for roast pheasant then use pheasant carcass, pigeon carcass for roast pigeon and so on and so forth. *Jus de turbot* is a strong sauce made from roast turbot bones and head, and for *jus de morue* use the wonderfully rich roasted bones of cod.

FOR 1 LITRE OF GOOD STRONG STOCK

5 kg veal or beef bones, cut into small pieces (ask your mate the butcher boy to help you)
7 large onions
12 black peppercorns
2 kg venison bones cut into small pieces (ask your game dealer to help you)

Place the veal/beef bones in a large baking tray and put it in a preheated oven at 180°C/gas 4. Leave the bones to roast for approx. 1½ hours until well browned. Place in a large pot with the excess fat well drained (saving it for later). Cover the bones well with fresh cold water and bring to the boil. Reduce the heat and skim any impurities from the surface of the stock – these fatty impurities should under no circumstances be boiled into the stock, the result will be muddy, murky, dull and greasy. Skimming is the most important part of the stock-making process, the more you skim the better it'll be... get it? So let's move on my lovelies.

The heat is now low and the stock should be just trembling, a faint simmer. Leave it like this for four hours. Skimming, removing the impurities whenever necessary, and adding a little fresh cold water every now and again. Halve and brown the onions carefully in a little of the fat from the baking tray and add to the stock together with the peppercorns. Leave the stock to simmer for a further hour. Remove the pot from the heat and leave the stock to rest for about half an hour. Then pass it through a fine sieve.

You now have good basic homemade veal or beef stock which you can continue to work on.

In order to make the stock ready for a venison sauce, brown the venison bones in a hot oven for about an hour. Pour the sieved stock into a clean pot with the browned venison bones and leave the stock simmering to infuse well for two hours. When you have approx. 1 litre of stock left, it has reduced sufficiently. Cool it down quickly. It should be kept cool or frozen in small portions.

Now the stock is ready, the sauce follows.

Sauce
– the genuine article

016

OUR SAUCE FOR VENISON
WITH DARK CHOCOLATE, DRIED FRUITS AND NUTS

100 ml fino sherry
200 ml red wine
200 ml strong veal/beef/venison stock
100 ml maple syrup
100 ml raspberry vinegar
½ tbsp finely chopped prunes
½ tbsp sultanas
½ tbsp dried cranberries
½ tbsp finely chopped dried apricots
½ tbsp raspberries
1 tsp toasted and finely chopped almonds
1 tsp finely chopped pistachio nuts
1 tsp finely chopped walnuts
½ tsp pink pepper

1 slice dried orange, chopped
1 tbsp chopped dark chocolate, from Scharffen Berger, if
  available
40 g cold butter in small cubes
Sea salt
Lemon

Pour the sherry into a small warm saucepan. Reduce to about
two tablespoons, pour over the wine and reduce to about four
tablespoons. Add the stock and leave the sauce to simmer for 10
minutes. In another small saucepan reduce the maple syrup to
about two tablespoons, add raspberry vinegar and reduce again
to half. Now you have a so-called *gastrique* (a sweet and sour
base to your sauce that gives it that certain tang). Pour the sauce
over into your gastrique. You should finally have about 200 ml
of finished sauce. Now add the dry ingredients, saving a little to
dress over the meat before serving.
Just before serving whisk the warm sauce with the small cubes of
cold butter, *monter au beurre*, giving the sauce its shine and the
rich rounded flavour. As said previously – from this point the sauce
must under no circumstances boil, otherwise it will curdle. Don't
forget to season the sauce with sea salt and maybe a little lift of
lemon juice.

TO SERVE
Mid-January and the shooting season is almost over for pheasant.
For pigeons and duck it's a little later. The same applies for the
Danish rabbits, hares, fallow and red deer.
As a final salute to sauce I thought it appropriate to finish the
season with a small dish from my last winter menu at The Paul – I
roasted a little venison fillet to a beautifully light pink, within
foaming brown butter flavoured with garlic, fresh thyme and a
single bay leaf. Leaving the meat to rest for a while, I prepared the
sauce salmis. This classic preparation method calls for the iron-
rich organs of the beast, chopped and whisked into my sauce,
enriching and giving a velvet tone, adding a whole new dimension.
Served with a little puree of smoked onion and the finest soured
green leaves of the tiniest sprouts that I could find. Happy small
guests, we again had that night.

PS – If you make sure the venison is at room temperature, when
you pan-roast it, it will not dry out so easily and a pink, pink result
is so much easier to obtain. This applies to any type of meat really.
Half an hour outside the fridge before you prepare your steak and
a most happy carnivore you will be.

Sauce
– the genuine article

016

Korsør

I have cooked for the some of the world's sharpest critics and food writers and the most gruesome, terrifying journalists, both from Denmark and abroad. I have had many a visit from the famous Michelin Guide Rouge folk. Prominent chef colleagues, the finest sommeliers and restaurateurs often ate at The Paul and judged our food, our wine and our service – as well as politicians, prime ministers and presidents. I have also had the great honour of cooking for Her Majesty the Queen of Denmark, her wonderful Prince Henrik and the entire royal family.

But the most nerve wracking dinner to date was in 1996 when I had to cook for my wife's Danish grandparents' diamond wedding celebrations – and thereby, at the same time, pass my test in her food-mad family's eyes. It was grandad Valdemar who chose the menu. He enjoyed food and was no novice in the kitchen and as far as the menu was concerned there would be no discussion, no element of surprise, no modern culinary intervention, just 'Shooting Star', traditional roast pork and ice cream terrine wrapped in marzipan with a chocolate sauce.

At the time I had not been in Denmark for too long and despite a thorough introduction to Danish food culture and cooking at home with my mother-in-law I had not yet met the legend that is 'Shooting Star', so I had to do a little research and was carried off to the south of Sjælland, where we ended up in a small market town. The town's most prestigious lunch restaurant was our destination. Here I would prepare myself for my first 'Shooting Star'. Grandad had placed the order before I had even managed to park the car. In came an enormous dish with boiled and fried fish and defrosted prawns, cheap mayonnaise seasoned with an even cheaper ketchup, iceberg salad, tomatoes, lemon curls, cress and some black coloured roe they had the cheek to call caviar. Everything piled up into a monster of a puff pastry case. How on earth would the diamond-aged guests manage three courses at the party, if this was just one of them?

We finished, just taking breath. But grandpapa wanted dessert, and after not too much pressure I chose a cheese, deep fried camembert with blackcurrant marmalade. Grandad didn't know the dish and joined me. He pierced his fork into the cheese, sending a jet of molten camembert straight up his tie and waistcoat – 'BLOODY HELL!' he screamed, 'this cheese is rotten!' shouted the semi-deaf elderly man in the tightly packed miniscule restaurant. I explained how it was made and that it was supposed to be like that, but to his dying day I don't think he was convinced.

After a little tweaking their diamond wedding went well, even though the rich and strong stock-based sauce, that my apprentice chef and I had prepared by the litre had to be diluted with at least as much water, after it was inspected by the eighty-something-year-old kitchen lady because she was convinced there was too little.

FOR FOUR

4 thick slices of sourdough bread
2 large handfuls of spinach, picked and washed
1 finely chopped shallot
4 large fillets of Dover sole with roe, if you are lucky
1 Danish lobster
Butter
A little plain white flour
2 large tomatoes from the vine, chopped and sautéed
    with a chopped shallot, then reduced with a little
    apple vinegar and sugar – seasoned, and blended to a
    ketchup
Sea salt and pepper
Juice and zest of a lemon
4 tbsp homemade mayonnaise made with olive oil
Caviar (the genuine article of course)

Toast the bread and keep it warm. Fry the spinach in a little butter or olive oil with the shallot, season with salt and pepper and keep warm. Cut the sole fillets in half and carefully poach four of these halves in a mixture of equal parts butter and lightly salted water (100 g butter to 100 ml water), just covering the fish. Coat the remaining four and the roe with plain flour, season with salt and fry crisp in butter.

Keep all the fillets warm. Boil the lobster in salted water. The tail should boil for two minutes, whereas the claws need half a minute more. Remove from the shell quickly and sear the lobster meat in a little browned butter with lemon zest. Mix your homemade tomato ketchup with the olive oil mayonnaise and season to taste.

Arrange a slice of bread with spinach, the one-of-each fillets of Dover sole, lobster and tomato'ed mayonnaise and topping with as much caviar as you like. And of course, a slice of lemon, elegantly folded on top. Beautiful as a shooting star!

A Danish classic *my way*

017

The smoked notes add a bit of mystery to this dish. The egg will acquire an almost earthy feel and suddenly an egg is not just an egg... also fantastic for drizzling over fresh steaming pasta or toasted sourdough. Mix with a bowl full of new boiled potatoes, just broken with the fingers before serving. Try the oil with brilliant vanilla ice cream, if you dare, maybe with a slice of apple pie.

Poached egg with smoked pine needle oil

018

SMOKED PINE NEEDLE OIL
1 litre mild olive oil or rapeseed oil
A few large but younger sprigs of new pine showing new spruce needles

Add the sprigs of pine needles to a heavy based saucepan and put them over a high heat. Leave until they start to smoke. They should be smoking strongly. Add the sprigs to a container or bottle with the oil and quickly secure the lid tightly. Place the container in a dark, cool place for a minimum of three days so the oil will be completely infused with the smoked properties from the pine.

SALAD WITH POACHED EGG
Super fresh large organic eggs
Small shallots, finely cut into rings
Salad leaves, rinsed
A little apple cider vinegar
Smoked pine oil
Sea salt and fresh pepper

Poach the eggs just how you like them. Quickly sauté the shallots and season. Dress the salad with a little apple cider vinegar, a couple of drops of pine needle oil, sea salt and fresh pepper. Arrange with egg and onion.

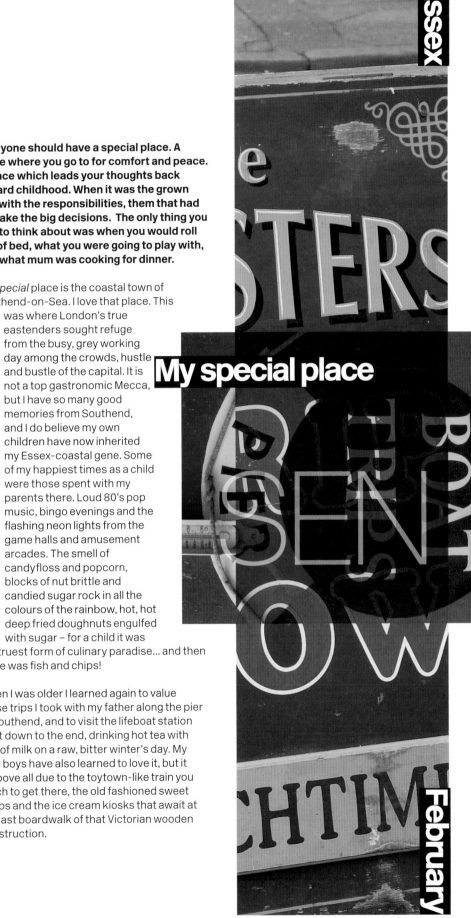

My special place

Everyone should have a special place. A place where you go to for comfort and peace. A place which leads your thoughts back toward childhood. When it was the grown ups with the responsibilities, them that had to make the big decisions. The only thing you had to think about was when you would roll out of bed, what you were going to play with, and what mum was cooking for dinner.

My *special* place is the coastal town of Southend-on-Sea. I love that place. This was where London's true eastenders sought refuge from the busy, grey working day among the crowds, hustle and bustle of the capital. It is not a top gastronomic Mecca, but I have so many good memories from Southend, and I do believe my own children have now inherited my Essex-coastal gene. Some of my happiest times as a child were those spent with my parents there. Loud 80's pop music, bingo evenings and the flashing neon lights from the game halls and amusement arcades. The smell of candyfloss and popcorn, blocks of nut brittle and candied sugar rock in all the colours of the rainbow, hot, hot deep fried doughnuts engulfed with sugar – for a child it was the truest form of culinary paradise... and then there was fish and chips!

When I was older I learned again to value those trips I took with my father along the pier at Southend, and to visit the lifeboat station right down to the end, drinking hot tea with lots of milk on a raw, bitter winter's day. My own boys have also learned to love it, but it is above all due to the toytown-like train you catch to get there, the old fashioned sweet shops and the ice cream kiosks that await at the last boardwalk of that Victorian wooden construction.

PIER MU

Fish pie

IE SHORE

019

Not so long ago I was asked to describe my last meal on this fine earth – where it would take place, how and when. I replied that I would sit at the end of the pier in Southend with my wife and my two wonderful boys. I would eat fish and chips or a good fish pie. I'd drink a glass of apple cider. It would be fantastic. Or as we say in Essex, that would be pukka!

FOR A FAMILY OF FOUR

50 g butter
50 g plain white flour
100 ml whipping cream
100 ml fish stock made from fish bones and the juice from the steamed shellfish

500 g fresh seasonal white fish fillets without skin, cut into large cubes – cod, haddock, pollock, plaice
500 g fresh shellfish, steamed, peeled and chopped into cubes, for example lobster, prawns, langoustine, mussels, cockles or scallops
1 tbsp chopped parsley
1 tbsp chopped chives
Sea salt and fresh pepper
Lemon
2 large baking potatoes, steamed, mashed and mixed with a little extra butter and grated cheddar cheese

Melt the butter, whisk in the flour and let it cook a little. Heat the cream and the stock together in the same saucepan and pour slowly over the flour, a little at a time, whisking continuously to prevent lumps. When the sauce is thick and shiny, remove it from the heat.

Most carefully fold in the fish, shellfish and the herbs, season well with salt, pepper and a little lemon juice. Divide among four bowls, or indeed pour into one large dish, loosely spoon the cheese'y mashed potatoes on top. Bake the pies at 180°C/gas 4 for 25 minutes, golden and luverly.

Serve with garden peas, knobbed with butter.

You know you want it...

Hot apple pie and cold clotted cream

020

God save the Queen. Things just don't get anymore British. Hot apple pie with cold clotted cream will adorn the buffet at my life's last meal. And it will have to be a buffet for the simple reason that I have too many favourite dishes for it to be any different. Lobster Thermidor, chilli'ed linguine frutti di mare, turbot fried in butter and moules marinières. A really good NYC cheeseburger, an enormous garlic-buttered grilled T-bone, fish and chips and my nan's roast leg of lamb. And for dessert vanilla ice cream with Passard's salted caramel, Michel Bras' chocolate fondant, Michel Michaud's Gateau Marcel... and as always I will have to save a little space for my beloved apple pie and cold clotted Cornish cream.

FOR FOUR, IF I AM AMONG THEM – FOR SIX, IF I AM NOT

8 large seasonal apples
100 g salted butter – depending on the apples' sweetness,
   depending of course on the type and season
Light brown cane sugar – muscovado works terrific
1 split vanilla pod
Juice and zest of a half lemon
1 portion puff pastry made from butter (and not margarine)
1 egg yolk

Wash the apples, cut and core them into large wedges. Melt the butter in a pan and add the apples, with the sugar and split, scraped vanilla. Brown lightly for five minutes and then add lemon juice and zest.

Roll out the puff pastry thickly, to fit your chosen baking dish. Add the apples to the buttered baking dish and cover with the puff pastry. Brush with egg yolk and sprinkle well with sugar. Bake at 180°C/gas 4 until the pie is crisp and golden, about 30-40 minutes. Serve with lashings of cold Cornish clotted cream.

Cockles from Leigh-on-Sea with malt vinegar & black pepper

021

Ten minutes before you arrive at Southend-on-Sea, just where the Thames looks out into the sea, and a little to the right, you will see a little Thomas the Tank Engine-like station. When I was a small boy my mum, dad and my little sister Sally and I would occasionally drive down to Leigh. It was a short trip of just over half an hour, but it always felt so holiday-like. Streets of small restaurants and cafes, dodgy maritime souvenir shops, a kiosk with plastic beach toys, Rossi ice cream and cups, and cups of tea. While my mum loved all things sweet, my dad always preferred the salt; the small stalls with fresh fish was what attracted him to the place. Boiled dressed crab with wedges of lemon, smoked mackerel, herrings, and the odd jellied eel. Small cooked shrimps, whelks and above all cockles, they were his favourite... today they are mine too. In those days they did nothing to them other than steam them, until they opened then they were drizzled with a little dark malt vinegar and seasoned with lots of freshly ground black pepper.

500 g completely fresh cockles per person
Malt or sherry vinegar
Freshly ground black pepper

Rinse the cockles thoroughly and steam them in salted water or just in sea water. The ones that open you can eat, discard the rest. Drizzle with vinegar, sprinkle with pepper and enjoy them as they are.

Happy picking folks!

Santiago de Compostela

At the top of Spain, to the left lies the holiest of holy, Santiago de Compostela; the capital of Spain's most important religious region of Galicia, where devout pilgrims stand side-by-side with tourists in the town's gazillion tapas bars.

One day I met my wife's cousin at the station of my hometown here in Denmark. He stood there in all his comfortable shoe and rucksacked glory, on his way to Valencia. From where he'd embark upon his 1600 km stroll to Santiago de Compostela in the north. 'But why?' I asked. 'Because I can', he replied, in a slightly Forrest Gump'ish tone.

That, I suppose, was a good enough explanation for me.

A couple of years ago I was at the food festival of Forum Gastronomique in Santiago de Compostela; a nerd driven nerdy trade fair for chefs, restaurateurs and wine folk alike. Meeting and deliberating, screaming and shouting. Breaking down, loving and breathing every aspect

A most culinary pilgrimage

SCQ

of foods and wines… *god I love a good nerd.*

I unpacked within the world's oldest hotel (according to their own assertion), the grand Hostal Dos Reis Catolicos, which is just up the road from Casa Marcelo. Marcelo Tejedor is a local gastro-hero, he heads a local elite force of new wave chefs who represent and take fierce pride in their new style of Galician gastronomy. Championing only very local raw materials, exposing them to new techniques inspired by the master that is El Bulli's own Ferran Adrià. I first met Marcelo a few years back on Mauritius, we got on immediately. It was being with Marcelo that had ignited the idea of this gastronomic pilgrimage to his hometown. The purpose of the journey was however, not the town's Gothic Batman's batcave of a cathedral, but the local markets, the ones with the freshest fish, Kobe-inspired beef from one of the nearby farms and the small family-owned, family-run restaurants of the old town.

I believe Marcelo would be proud of this little black number. Simple, but carefully thought through. Dark and full of depth, just like the man himself, and not completely unlike his hometown. I can still remember one of the dishes Marcelo composed on Mauritius: A thick slice of fresh red-skinned snapper poached in his own, bought-from-home olive oil and perfumed with grilled red pepper. With this an intensely reduced stock made from the beast's head, olive oil and lemon. He cooled and whisked it into a sort of fish mayonnaise. Garlic'ly delicious and gothic'ly diabolical!

FOR FOUR

PICKLED TRUMPET MUSHROOMS
1 handful of black trumpet mushrooms – washed, trimmed and sorted
100 ml good olive oil
1 clove garlic, chopped
100 ml sherry vinegar
2 tbsp sugar

6 medium sized fresh calamari, octopus or squid, about 50 g pp
1 large onion, finely sliced
2 cloves garlic, crushed
Olive oil
2 tbsp fresh breadcrumbs
½ deseeded red chilli, chopped fine
Sea salt
Lemon juice
Sherry vinegar

Dried octopus crackers (available from Chinese and Japanese grocers)

SAUCE
100 ml strong chicken stock
100 ml strong fish and/or shellfish stock
50 g cold butter
1 tsp squid ink
Sherry vinegar
Sea salt

Squid within Squid. The new black

022

Start by pickling the mushrooms. Quickly sauté the trimmed and cleaned mushrooms in the hot olive oil with garlic. Add sherry vinegar and sugar, simmer gently for five minutes. Let infuse for at least two hours.

Prepare and wash the squid thoroughly. Cut two of the bodies and the tentacles from all six squid, into fine strips. Brown the onion and garlic in olive oil until golden. Add the finely sliced squid. Leave to sauté for a further 15 minutes until tender, remove from the heat. Fold together with the breadcrumbs and fine chilli, season with sea salt, lemon and sherry vinegar. Leave to cool for a while, and then stuff the four remaining squid bodies with the mixture. Secure with small wooden skewers and leave to set in the fridge.

For the sauce – boil the stocks together and reduce to about half. Remove the pot from the heat and whisk in the cold butter. Whisk in the squid ink and season to taste with sherry vinegar, lemon and sea salt. Warm the stuffed squid well through the intensely flavoured, deep black squid inked sauce. Serve with the pickled mushrooms and octopus crackers.

A spicy sweet-sour Spanish stew served at garden temperature. Everything could in fact be more or less be served à l'escabèche – a typically Spanish way of marinating or preparing food. Here it is the wonderful Danish calf sweetbreads from northern Jutland together with the salty, creamy Limfjord oysters, whose rich consistency contrasts well with the sour, fresh pickled vegetables and herbs. Try escabèche'd vegetables with red gurnard, weaver or mullet, lobster and langoustine, and even with a piece of grilled rib-eye, or grilled aubergine, asparagus or tofu, its fab.

FOR FOUR

ESCABÈCHE
100 ml white wine or apple vinegar
100 ml white wine
100 ml mineral water
100 ml really good olive oil
1 fennel bulb, finely sliced
2 shallots, finely sliced
4 cloves garlic, crushed
1 finely sliced carrot
4 spring onions, sliced
2 large Spanish red peppers, grilled and skin removed, then cut into strips
A little fresh thyme, rosemary and oregano
2 fresh bay leaves
2 large tomatoes cut into a large concassé
Zest and juice of ½ lemon
Sea salt

200 g trimmed calf sweetbreads, soaked overnight in fresh cold water, refrigerated
8 large Limfjord oysters
A little flour, butter and olive oil for frying the sweetbreads
Fresh herbs and edible herb flowers, if available

Bring the vinegar, wine, water and olive oil to a simmer. Add the fennel, shallot, garlic, carrot, onions and grilled peppers. Throw in the herbs and bay leaves and simmer gently for 5 minutes. Remove from the heat and add the tomatoes, lemon and season well.

Sprinkle the trimmed sweetbreads with sea salt and fresh pepper, leave for half an hour. Roll them in the flour and fry them, crisp and golden brown in olive oil, finishing with a knob of fresh butter.

Remove the large oysters from their shells and very quickly indeed sear them on only one side for no more that 20 seconds in a super hot non-stick pan.

Serve the sweetbreads and oysters with the warm marinade with the vegetables.

Himmerland calf sweetbreads with Limfjord oysters à l'escabèche

023

'Txangurro' spider crab

024

Galicia is home to the treasures of the sea. If you're not into fish and shellfish you should probably go somewhere else for your holiday. The local lamprey is revered and is considered the utmost of delicacies. It comes from the rivers around Santiago, and it reminds me a bit of a really brassed off eel and a completely psycho pike. The head looks as if it has been sawn off and replaced by two sets of real evil nasty Hannibal Lecter teeth that are mounted onto one end of the fish's monstrous torso. To boot, this bloodsucking-super swimmer costs more money than you can shake-a-stick-at when you ask for it in the local market, and much much, more when it arrives prepared in olive oil, garlic and lemon in the town's many restaurants. I regret to confess that I simply and most politely declined a chance to taste the beast when I was offered a plate in one of the town's local eating houses. Instead, I made do with the local spider crab followed by a rather large grilled Kobe-looking veal chop. Everything washed down with an excellent vino from the area of Duoro, produced actually by a mate of mine, a Danish lad by the name of Peter, lovely bloke he is too.

FOR TWO HUNGRY CHEFS AND A RESTAURANT CRITIC

1 large live spider crab
50 ml olive oil
2 large onions, finely sliced
4 garlic cloves, crushed
1 small glass Spanish brandy
1 glass of dry sherry
Sea salt and freshly ground black pepper
Sherry vinegar
Lemon juice

Wash the crab extremely well and plunge into boiling salted water, simmer for ten minutes, leaving the crab to rest within the water for a further ten minutes.
Remove all the meat from the body and claws, remembering to retain all of the intensely flavoured juices from the crab, this will later create the base flavour of the sauce.

Soften and lightly colour the sliced onions and garlic in the warmed olive oil. Flambé with brandy and let it reduce slightly. Add the sherry and let it again reduce. Add the crab juices, simmer for two minutes. Add the crab meat, stirring carefully and season with sea salt, fresh pepper, sherry vinegar and lemon juice. Serve in the cleaned shell, with a touch more olive oil, good bread and lightly dressed salad leaves.

Mauritius

A while ago I was sitting at home, staring out the window at the rain soaked day, miserable and grey. The phone rang and a friendly man asked if I would like to fly to sunny Mauritius, to take part in the food festival for the late Bernard Loiseau – an annual event held in honour of the multi-Michelin starred chef who most sadly left us to cook on the great stove in the sky, back in 2003. The idea was to bring six chefs from one-star Michelin restaurants to the exotic ex-French colonial island to inspire and coach the local up-and-coming chefs, who would then in turn compete with each other for the title of Young Chef of the Year.

The chef I was assigned to inspire was Aviraj, Avi to his friends. He was 27 but looked a perfectly fresh 17, of Indian heritage, with dark skin, pure, piercing white eyes and a newly pressed chef's jacket with the name of the French master chef on his left breast pocket. Together we would chop, sauté, bake and create. We decided on a couple of dishes which were to portray an edible gastronomic image of Mauritius. Our first dish was *Mauritius Oceanique*, sweet local carrots with finely cut raw shrimp, watercress essence and a lighter than light shrimp bisque. Following that the island's creation, *Mauritius Volcanique*, local lobster roasted with pink grapefruit, pomegranate and fresh palm heart. And finally *Mauritius Vert*, a picture of the island today. Grilled red tuna embedded by local green herbs, palm heart pureed with saffron root and a chutney made with local limes, green mango and pipangill (a sort of cross between a cucumber and a courgette).

Unfortunately brave Avi didn't win the competition that year. The prize of a European trip eluded him also the year after, mentored that time by my great friend and colleague Thomas Rode Andersen of Copenhagen's Kong Hans fame. But we had a wonderful couple of short weeks in each other's company.
A year later Avi finally got his revenge, and got his ticket to Europe, to France to be precise. There he worked within the kitchen of a most grandly starred restaurant with unfortunately some rather mixed experiences to follow. After a few turbulent and very unfriendly weeks I arranged for him to fly to Copenhagen. Avi stayed at home with me and mine, and that young man graced my kitchen. We also managed a trip up to my old stamping ground of Søllerød Kro. A wonderful dinner we had, I don't think Avi has ever seen and eaten so much food in his entire life.

Homage to Bernard Loiseau

Avi's red salt fish curry

025

FOR FOUR PEOPLE

1 tsp fennel seeds
1 tbsp mustard seeds
1 cinnamon stick
1 tsp cumin
2 tbsp garam masala
1 tbsp tandoori masala
1 tbsp mango powder
4 tbsp vegetable oil
2 onions, chopped
4 cloves garlic, sliced
2 red peppers, grilled, seeds and skin removed
1 tbsp chopped fresh ginger
1 fennel bulb, sliced
1 red chilli, sliced
8 tomatoes concassé
1 tbsp tomato puree
500 ml water
1 kg salted cod, soaked overnight in cold water, which should be
    replaced frequently
Lime juice
1 bunch spring onions, sliced
1 bunch fresh coriander

Very carefully, fry all of the dry spices gently for five minutes in the
vegetable oil. Add onions, garlic, peppers, ginger, fennel and chilli,
sauté for 10 minutes. Add the fresh tomatoes, tomato puree and
water. Simmer under a lid for an hour.

Cut the rinsed salt-cod into large cubes and stir into the deep red
curry. Simmer most gently for 30 minutes. The remaining salt in
the cod should flavour the curry nicely, but correct it if needed with
sea salt. Freshen the curry with lime juice, spring onions and fresh
coriander. Serve with hot naan and steamed basmati rice.

Miss you Avi.

I learned much from my pal Avi and Mauritius. One of my last lessons is that you can't hold a real Mauritian beach party without inviting Old Bob. Ancient Bob, as he should rightly be called, and his wife have a battered barbecue-wagon tied with string to the back of their old Ford. But that's often how things are my friends – my old Barbour is just perfect, my old Leica I love and my old Land Rover I miss with every breath… old is good, old is cool.

My last night on the bounty island was undoubtedly the highlight of my short trip. We were invited to the beach just before the sun went down. Lots of lovely smiling faces, prominent guests and sponsors, resort bosses and the young chefs alike drank chilled champagne and the freshest of juiced fruits. An array of small kitchens were lined up along the sand, ready for this ocean-side gala dinner… and down at the end was Old Bob alongside his wife. Both dressed in the whitest, most pristine chef's jackets (a hundred years old, yes, but still the whitest chefs jackets I have ever seen), and wearing frayed old panama straw hats. On the grill they had the finest honey-glazed, slow-roasted suckling pig which they served with local pineapple, glazed in spiced caramel. My recipe, using lamb, is a little simpler than Old Bob's but no matter what, please promise me that you'll carry your finished result down to your local beach on a late summer night, and dip your pinkies in the water… weather permitting of course.

FOR EIGHT

3 large pineapples
200 ml white wine or apple cider vinegar
500 g honey
2 split red chillies
1 tbsp chopped fresh ginger
8 star anise
2 cinnamon sticks
1 split vanilla pod
Sea salt
4 kg trimmed, rolled and tied necks of beautiful lamb – 4/5 pieces

Day one
Make a salt brine of 500 g salt to 1 litre of water, boiled together and cooled well. Immerse the tied lamb necks into the chilled brine, cover and refrigerate overnight.

Peel one pineapple, remove the core and blend to a pulp. Pour this into a large heavy saucepan with the vinegar, honey, chilli, ginger, star anise, cinnamon and vanilla, and warm it through. Season lightly with the sea salt and cool completely.

Day two
Lift the salted necks from the brine, dry and place into the spiced pineapple sauce. Cover, refrigerate overnight if possible.

Day three
Light your grill. When the coals are ready push them over to one side, you'll need to grill the necks on the other side of the grill, using the indirect heat from the hot coals. A circular type grill/barbecue, with a lid is perfect for this. Place the marinated necks of lamb onto the grill and gently, carefully roast them. Basting with the marinade, they'll take about two hours to reach their sticky, gooey melt-in-the-mouth, tender result.

Peel and cut the remaining pineapples into large pieces and grill them over the hot coals. Serve the tender spiced barbecued necks of lamb with the remaining warmed sauce and the grilled pineapple.

PS; can be also transported very well when stuffed into a hollowed-out baguette !!

Neck of pork braised, on a beach, with pineapple

026

Avi's *Mauritius Volcanique*. I use our Danish black lobsters but large prawns, langoustine or langouste are just as good. Bon appetit my lovely ones.

FOR FOUR

2 fresh live Danish black lobsters
4 tbsp olive oil
1 clove garlic, crushed
½ split chilli
Segments from one ruby grapefruit
1 small handful macadamia nuts
Sea salt

Kill swiftly, cut the lobsters in half, and crack the claws with the back of a heavy knife. Brown the lobster tail for two minutes in hot olive oil with garlic and chilli (the claws for three minutes). Throw in the grapefruit segments and the macadamia nuts. Season with the sea salt. Serve immediately, in or out of the shell.

Lobster, pink grapefruit & macadamia nuts

027

Desserts and sweet creations are not the most popular items on exotic islands. The local markets of Mauritius are full of fresh berries, seasonal fruits and coconuts, the islanders enjoy fruit salads, ice creams, sorbets, smoothies, milkshakes and spiced Indian lassies. Sugar-injected sweets and cream cakes are for tourists only.

However this little tropical 'jelly' has graced my menus for a few years now. The grilled caramelised tones from the acidic lemon, work perfectly with the smooth, intense almond-like perfume from the tonka bean from Mauritius's neighbouring island of Madagascar.

Grilled lemon gel with tonka bean sugar

028

30-40 SMALL GELS

12 large untreated lemons (500 g finished, sieved lemon pulp)
400 g sugar + 100 g
75 g glucose
30 g pectin

You will need a sugar thermometer for this recipe.

Cut the lemons through lengthwise and place them with the flesh side down on a hot non-stick pan. Caramelise until dark brown, bordering on blackened, this will take about 8-10 minutes. Place in an ovenproof dish and put in a hot oven at 180°C/gas 4 for 30 minutes, until completely soft and the inner flesh is soft to a spoon.

Cool slightly, but whilst still warm press the juice from lemons through a fine sieve, retaining every single drop of this now fantastic, concentrated, lightly caramelised lemon pulp.

Warm the 500 g lemon pulp with the 400 g of sugar and glucose, stirring continuously until the sugar has dissolved completely. Stir in the pectin and the remaining 100 g of sugar. Turn up the heat so the mixture reaches 106°C (for this you will now need the sugar thermometer). Leave to boil gently for 5-6 minutes. Pour the mixture into a plastic container, cover and leave refrigerated overnight. When needed cut the jelly into small pieces and coat in tonka sugar. The finished gel itself stores very well, refrigerated without the sugar.

TONKA SUGAR
50 g sugar
¼ tsp citric acid
¼ tsp finely grated tonka bean – sourced from specialist spice dealers

Mix the three ingredients and put the sugar into an airtight container. Leave to infuse for 24 hours before use.

Tokyo

外神田四丁目田代会　毘

My base in the centre of Tokyo was Ginza, I moved warily amongst the city's 12 million people. I had expected a more chaotic atmosphere – but no, the architects and city planners of Imperial Tokyo have liberally but most deliberately placed green areas between their cutting-edge constructions of concrete, steel and glass. The city is beautiful, wonderful, intriguing. The atmosphere most friendly; I love the way the Japanese are, their actions, their mannerisms. Throughout Japan I have met only the most lovely, intelligent, creative, interesting people. The Japanese culture and the Japanese day is curious to say the least, on the one hand so ultra-modern with their mini mobiles, electric cars, tip-top fashion sense and crazy, cartoon-Manga figures. On the Yen's flip-side they appear so true to their age-old generation bound traditions. Their extreme politeness and natural respect, not only for each other, but for us tourists alike. Family Sunday traditions, their very public garden parties and their phenomenal eating habits.

In 2007 Michelin published for the first time their little red guide to Tokyo. The city was straightaway awarded 191 stars – every place mentioned had at least one star. It sounded unreal, almost absurd, but don't forget that there are around 16,000 eating houses in the centre of Tokyo town.

I set out one morning to try one of the absolutely best restaurants in the city. The place had received three stars and has a cult status within the city's gastronomic inner-circle. Ringing helped not, e-mailing proved to be just as hopeless, a more direct approach was obviously called for, a black cab. After my most friendly taxi driver had spent almost 25 minutes calling to his nearest and dearest to get help to trace the place, I jumped out of his pristine polished taxi actually none-the-wiser, and set about trying to find the restaurant myself. After almost an hour I found the building, don't ask how, I just did. In the tacky mirrored lobby were at least 80 small buffed brass name plates; of the 80 signs there were three letters which were not printed in Japanese, *B.I.F. B.I.F* was also the only letter I could understand when I scribbled down the name and address of this infamous establishment. It apparently means cellar. I went downstairs to the lower floor, finding not a smart cellar with chandeliers and marble floors, but an old cellar with dusty flat-tired bicycles, empty boxes and a couple of used dustbin bags. I thought 'yes', wrong again. But at the end of the small corridor stood a tiny door, left just open with a handwritten, decidedly wonky, name plate hanging upon it. Very gently I knocked on the door and out came a little chef – the conversation that took place goes a little like this…

He smiled, bowed.
I said 'Hello'.
He smiled again.
'A table for one, please?'
He smiled again, bowed once again, and then gently shook his head.
'Err…Please, a table for one, for lunch?'
He smiled again and said nothing.→

My Japanese spring

NRT

Suddenly a hand appeared from behind the door holding a tiny piece of folded paper. The handwritten message read…

'Welcome to restaurant. Our restaurant is full house. We are ALWAYS full house.
Please – you will never get table. We are always full restaurant!
Thank you.
No English. Goodbye.'

The small chef bowed and disappeared, with his folded paper note, behind the little wooden door. I took a photo of the door and left. Certainly the most surreal experience of my short life, and definitely the strangest event I have encountered at any restaurant establishment with three twinkly, sparkly Michelin stars.
I later discovered that behind that little wooden door, is a tiny bar with only room for eight guests at any one time. The chef had cut sashimi, prepared sushi and perfected his form of Japanese cuisine for more than fifty-odd years. He is cult chef number one in Tokyo and he is *The Man*. Now that this phantom-like figure has been internationally outed by the awarding of his three stars, he has become world famous. And rumour has it that he is none too happy with all the global media attention that comes with his new found fame.
Next time I'll book with a Japanese surname – anybody know the Japanese for Cunningham?

A sunny Sunday afternoon in the gardens of the Imperial Palace, full of young families. Their antique grandparents resting on the warm grass under the old blossoming cherry and plum trees. While mother pours hot green tea and father cuts the cake, the Japanese love their cakes, and the sweeter, the better. Small children play on the perfectly kept lawns with the latest smash-hit Japanese toys. I bought boxes of the newest Gundan robot-warrior-samurai home with me for my son Christian. If the complete truth was told, I think I actually acquired them for myself – he was not amused when he discovered that I had borrowed one of them for the photograph.

2 tbsp water
4 tbsp sugar
8 juicy plums, cubed
200 g butter
Seeds from 1 vanilla pod
225 g icing sugar
250 g marzipan
4 eggs, separated
100 g potato flour
50 g plain white flour
75 g ground almonds
1 tsp baking powder

In a super-clean pan, boil the water and sugar together and reduce slightly to a light caramel. Add the plums and simmer for five minutes. Remove the saucepan from the heat and leave to cool.

Beat the butter and sugar together with the vanilla seeds until soft and light. In another bowl soften the marzipan and beat in the egg yolks, one by one, fold the two mixtures together.

Gently fold in the sieved potato flour, sieved plain flour, ground almonds and baking powder. Whisk the egg whites stiff and carefully fold into the mixture.

Fold the plums and juices carefully into the batter, and pour into a well buttered, sugared cake tin. Bake the cake in a hot oven at 180°C/gas 4 for one hour.

Enjoy on the lawn with hot tea, family and friends.

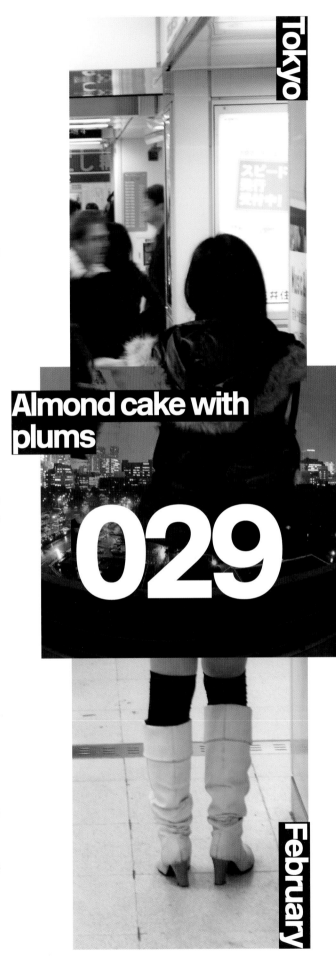

Almond cake with plums

029

Maybe the combination seems odd. But when tasted it makes perfect sense. Simple and too-the-point. To be washed down with a good Japanese beer.

FOR FOUR

100 ml Japanese teriyaki sauce
1 tbsp brown sugar
70 g fillet of smoked eel per person
Yuzu juice from your local Japanese supermarket
20 strawberries
1 handful of baby beetroot leaves

Reduce the teriyaki sauce with brown sugar to a sticky glaze. Slice the smoked eel and sear quickly in a very hot non-stick pan. Glaze the eel carefully with the warm teriyaki sauce. Sharpen the taste with a little yuzu. Serve with the sweet strawberries and beetroot leaves.

PS; Yes, I know its February in the book and strawberries are not out yet – you'll just have to wait my lovelies.

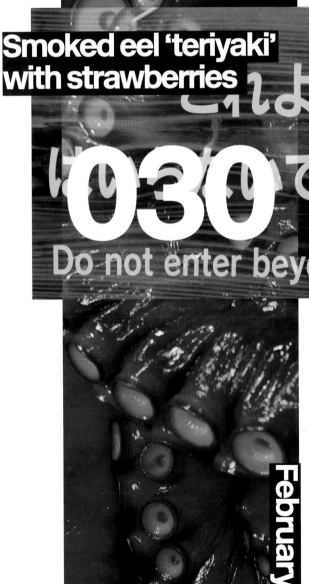

Smoked eel 'teriyaki' with strawberries

030

Do not enter beyon

I hate to be this positive, but everything about that trip to Japan made a deep and lasting impression on me and my soul. My frugal, boxed and most spartan hotel room with a view, looked out over a high-tech red and white version of the Eiffel tower to one side, and an ancient untouched, unspoilt temple with a matching cemetery to the other. The almost embarrassingly well-kept taxicabs, driven by white-cotton-gloved drivers, sitting on hand-embroidered, granny-crocheted seat covers, also stitched in brilliant, blinding white. The way they greet and converse. The carefully studied exchange of business cards. The much respected Sumo with their handprints in the concrete sidewalks and their enormous competition stadium perched alongside yet another pre-history temple. The order and the controlled chaos...and of course the food.

The great fish market at Tsukiji rocks and rolls twenty-four-seven. For a passionate chef, the World's 8th Wonder – hundreds of tuna and locally caught bonito lined up for auction, bidders with small flashlights on their knees, examining with surgeon-like expertise. Wetsuit-clad workers wield their super-sharp weapons of choice, filleting fish with deadly accuracy, full length *katanas* sharpened to razors. I now know where all the Samurai disappeared to. Within the market's many passages lay one of Japanese gastronomy's best kept secrets – the eating-houses of Tsukiji are quite simply beyond belief. Opening their wooden shutters in the middle of the night (or is it early morning?), their hand-painted curtains bid warm welcome to a world of fishy pleasure. Still pulsating sea urchin roe poised upon warm secretly-seasoned rice. Steamed crab to be dipped in the darkest ponzu vinegar dressings, whilst freshwater river eel are grilled crisp over glowing hot coals, teriyaki'ed to boot. The market sushi was some of the best I have ever tasted. To be sitting, and sharing sake with the country's former silver-fox prime minister really put the cherry on top of my blossom-perfumed cake... making it nigh-on impossible for me to order sashimi, sushi, actually almost anything Japanese outside that wonderful country, spoilt I most certainly am.

FOR FOUR HUNGRY SUMO-LOVERS

MISO CRÈME
300 g mayonnaise, preferably homemade
3 tbsp toasted sesame oil
1 tbsp brown miso paste (it should not be the sweet version)
Sea salt
Yuzu

2 nice peaches
2 kg king crab
A little fresh seaweed – ask your deli
Fresh herbs

Start with the crème. Flavour the mayonnaise with sesame oil and miso paste, season with sea salt and yuzu.

Blanch the peaches in boiling water, refresh in iced, and skin them. Slice into smaller pieces. Leave to rest (un-chilled) until needed.

Boil the crab in well salted water for three minutes. Remove from the water and cool a little, then cut the meat from the shell using a pair of scissors to clip open the shelled arms. Lightly sear the meat in a super-hot non-stick pan and serve warm with peaches, seaweed, fresh herbs and the miso crème.

Red king crab, peach & miso

031

Well sourced ingredients from trusted suppliers and producers is key to the success of my restaurant. My nine-year relationship with 'Jesper-the-fish' results in only the very best being landed at my kitchen door. Mester Christensen is indeed the Meatman of Copenhagen's Meat-Town; I have been friends and a loyal customer of that beautiful butcher-boy for 13 long years now. GreenRonnie comes with our gorgeous vegetables and one of the other members of our brave most motley-crew is the young Mr.Woolly Wootten, a friendly British shepherd tending to his herd in the south of Sjælland. David's lamb is the sweetest, the most tender, the best... in my humble opinion.

Wootten lamb with salted lumpfish roe

032

FOR FOUR

175 g lamb per person – rump, rack, fillet, liver, kidney, sweetbreads if you can get them!
Sea salt and fresh black pepper
A little fresh seaweed
A little crisp dried fresh seaweed
100 g fresh salted lumpfish roe

DRESSING
Highest quality Japanese soy
Toasted sesame oil
Mirin
Yuzu juice

Season the lamb well, and roast it as you like it. Plate with fresh seaweed, dried seaweed and salted lumpfish roe. Dress with a little soy, sesame oil, mirin and yuzu (1 to 1, to 1 to 1).

Serve with steamed seasoned Japanese rice.

Spring

Miami

Miami is in a league of its own. Thrice now I have crossed the choppy Atlantic, to finish up at sunny Miami Beach. It is plastic... *Plastic fantastic*.

The architecture really belongs in a splendid and lavish Tim Burton film. Houses and hotels are painted in everything from pink to baby blue, from lime green to *a lighter shade of pale.*
The first time I was there it required a little adjusting between the daytime's ultra laid back near-Cuban pace, to the evening's hectic silicone-boogie-woogie-neon lights from the clubs and bars. Juices, tacos, dogs – fresh cut iced cerviche, super hamburgers, malted milkshakes and super-bitter blackened coffees are offered on every street corner.
To escape the streets, Christian my trusted friend and head-chef, quickly found a most tranquil escape within the back garden of the Hotel Raleigh on Collins Avenue. Built by the infamous American architect L. Murray Dixon back in the 1940's, with its original art-deco designed rooms, fleur-de-lys pool and *über-chic* clientele, it is a throwback to the days when the likes of the Hemingways and Garbos hung out with Gables, Presleys and Deans. The Monroes chilled with cool mojitos inspiring the newer generations – the Clooneys, Pitts, Gagas and *The Cunninghams*.

Raleigh lobster with bitter salad and lychees

033

FOR TWO PEOPLE

2 live not-too-large lobsters, each about 250 g
Melted butter
Sea salt and fresh black pepper
12 fresh lychees
Frisée salad – warm, and picked. *Only using the pale yellow leaf,*
green being too bitter
Lemon
Paul's house dressing (see below)

Peel the lychees and prepare the salad, placing only the pale yellow
leaves into a bowl of iced water until needed.
Kill the lobsters and cook whole, in boiling, well salted water for
four minutes. Remove from the saucepan and leave to rest for 10
minutes. Cut the body in half, clip open the joints and crack the
claws with the back of a heavy knife. Plate the lobsters and brush
most liberally with plenty of melted butter, a good squeeze of
lemon, and season with sea salt and fresh ground pepper.
Serve the lobsters with lychees, dress the frisée leaves lightly with
the house dressing.

PAUL'S HOUSE DRESSING
50 ml white wine vinegar
100 ml olive oil
100 ml vegetable oil, such as grapeseed oil
1 tbsp Dijon mustard
1 tbsp crème fraîche 38%
Sea salt and pepper
Lemon juice

Whisk the vinegar, oils, mustard and crème fraîche together well.
Season with sea salt, fresh pepper and lemon juice. Pour the
dressing into a bottle and place in the fridge, leaving to infuse for
one hour... using of course at room or garden temperature.

In Miami anything is possible. I've seen silicone zeppelins on well-worn grannies, blokes in their 60's skating in leopard skin Speedos, and many a flossing-cotton used to cover the most sunned areas of skin. Food-wise there are funky Cuban creations crossed with Japanese majesty and the finest of French *haute cuisine* meeting the fire of Old Mexico. The most wonderful culinary experience I have experienced in Crockett and Tubbs' backyard though, remains to be the delightful, delectable lack of fatty fast food.

This recipe is dedicated to the gastronomic-vices of Miami!

FOR FOUR

4 pieces of smoked eel each about 60 g
4 pieces foie gras, also about 60 g pp
1 fennel bulb and top, most finely cut and placed into iced water
1 shallot, very finely sliced
2 tbsp mayonnaise, made with olive oil
2 drops of white truffle oil – yes drops!
Sea salt and fresh black pepper
My barbecue sauce – please see below
1 small fresh truffle – type depending on the season
English candied liquorice – from specialist spice shops

Sear the eel well on the skin side only, in a very hot non-stick pan. Season the foie gras pieces and pan-roast them golden brown on both sides. Dress the fennel and the shallot lightly with the mayonnaise, adding only two drops of the white truffle oil – season with a touch of sea salt and fresh ground pepper.
Brush the plates with the barbecue sauce, arrange the hot eel, foie gras and coleslaw. Grate or slice the truffle on top, finishing with the finely grated liquorice (a microplane being perfect for this task).

HONEY-GINGER-BARBECUE SAUCE
250 ml ketchup
150 ml Worcestershire sauce
150 ml HP sauce
125 g honey
250 g brown sugar
1 tsp freshly grated ginger
½ red chilli
¼ pineapple, cubed

Bring all of the sauce ingredients to a gentle boil, reduce the heat and simmer for 45 minutes, blend fine and cool. If you can wait, leave the sauce to infuse for a few days, refrigerated.

Grilled smoked eel, foie gras & barbecue sauce with fennel-truffle-coleslaw

034

Chocolate sorbet

035

It doesn't often happen with me, but it had to be done. I sent back the *rock solid-over-whipped-not-so-fantastic* chocolate mousse that I'd ordered at my favourite hotel in Miami. Chocolate sorbet arrived instead, it was quite simply superb. Simple, sublime. And so is this! I nicked the recipe from pal Christophe Dufau, *chef française* of Les Baccanhales, Vence and the beautiful gardens of Provence.

ABOUT 1 LITRE

1 litre mineral water
80 g cocoa powder
60 g glucose
340 g dark chocolate, finely chopped
50 ml dark rum
¼ tsp sea salt
1 sheet leaf gelatine dissolved in water

Boil the water and leave to simmer for five minutes with cocoa powder and glucose. Remove from the heat, whisk and dissolve the finely chopped chocolate, rum and sea salt. Add the leaf gelatine to the warm sorbet base. When completely smooth, pass through a fine sieve. Cool the base thoroughly and run it in an ice-cream machine.

You can't drive the Southern states without bumping into a bowl of chowder or two. About 45 minutes out of Miami, on the way down to the glamorous sunny Florida Keys, you'll pass the greened swamplands of the Everglades. Here you will find all kinds of indigenous animals that the locals throw into their chowder – from the most ferocious alligators to snapping crocodiles, huge river snakes and giant frogs, you name it! Luckily chowder is one of those recipes where you can decide yourself what to throw into the pot. This recipe is based on mussels and shrimps but you are naturally free to improvise along the way.

FOUR TO SIX HILLBILLYBOYS *OR INDEED GIRLS*

2 onions, sliced fine
2 cloves garlic, crushed
½ tsp fennel seeds, toasted and lightly crushed
½ green chilli, sliced
2 tbsp butter
1 large baking potato, peeled and cut into small cubes
Sweet corn kernels, from 2 cobs
400 ml roast chicken stock, made from the carcass of a roast chicken
200 ml milk
500 g mussels – blue mussels or cockles, washed thoroughly with no traces of sand
8 large prawns, or langoustines. Peeled, but keep the shells
Sea salt and fresh black pepper
Key lime juice – or lemon/lime mixed juices if you can't get key lime juice
Vegetable oil
Parsley and tarragon, washed and chopped

Corn chowder, mussels & prawns

036

Lightly colour the onions, garlic, fennel seed and chilli in hot butter. Add potato cubes and sweet corn and leave to sweat a little longer. Add the stock and milk and leave to simmer very gently for 15 minutes. The soup should not boil as the milk will curdle.

Add the cleaned mussels and prawns cut into large pieces. Simmer the soup most gently for a further ten minutes, until all the mussels have opened. Discard any that do not open. Season with sea salt, fresh ground pepper and the key lime juice.

Deep fry the shrimp shells in hot vegetable oil, until crisp and golden. Drain the crisp shells well over kitchen paper, dress well with fine sea salt. Serve the chowder with fresh chopped parsley and tarragon, and the crisp fried shrimp shells.

There are thousands of different recipes for this Florida classic. It is rich, creamy and delicious. And every café, diner, restaurant or eatery worth its salt in Miami, and its surroundings has their own homemade version of it. I must confess I have probably tasted most of them – Key Lime pie by Joe's Stone Crabs being my favourite.

EIGHT OR TEN SUNNY MIAMI BEAUTIES

20 digestive biscuits, finely crushed
150 g melted butter
300 ml fresh lime juice – or indeed key-lime juice if you are in the area
200 g sugar
2 large leaves of gelatine
2 eggs, separated into yolks and whites
250 ml double cream
100 g mascarpone
Zest of 1 lime

Mix the crushed biscuits with the butter and press the mixture into a round greased baking tray – just like a cheesecake. Bring the lime juice to the boil and reduce by half, add the sugar, dissolve and remove from the heat. Add the softened gelatine. Whisk the egg yolk well and whip the whites until most stiff. In a new bowl, whisk the cream and the mascarpone until they form soft peaks.

Carefully fold the egg yolks, egg whites and the cream-mascarpone into the now cool lime juice mixture. Add the finely grated zest of lime. Pour the cream over the biscuit base, cover the pie and leave refrigerated overnight – giving the pie time to set and giving the lime aromas time to infuse throughout the cream.

Key Lime pie

037

Yes, ok… it's probably a little *Desperate Housewives*. A small wooden house with white painted window frames, and a white painted picket-fence. A swing sofa on the veranda. Green grassed, well-flowered garden and an enormous *f**k-off, 2 litre, twincam, 4x4 intergalactic Ford thrice-turboblockbuster* in the driveway. Get the picture? Washed down with an iced jug of homemade lemonade. Welcome to the American dream, folks!

1 LITRE'ISH LEMONADE CONCENTRATE

Juice 8 organic lemons, zest from 4
600 ml water
200 g cane sugar

MINTED GINGER LEMONADE FOR FOUR
Ice cubes
½ lemon, thinly sliced
4 slices of fresh ginger
1 large sprig mint
200 ml lemonade concentrate
800 ml ice cold mineral water

For the concentrate – boil the ingredients, place in a clean sterilised bottle with a good lid and leave to cool overnight.

Half fill a chilled jug with ice cubes, throw in the lemon slices, sliced ginger and the mint. Pour over the lemonade concentrate and top up with mineral water. Mix well and serve in iced glasses, fresh from the freezer. Rub the edges of the glass with lemon for extra effect.

This recipe can be made with lime instead of lemon, whilst adding a good splash of dark rum… *Cheers Hemingway!*

Homemade mint lemonade
– *spiked if you wish*

038

Ripe melon in the height of its season is wonderful.
It's as refreshing as an ice lolly and a tad healthier.
To accentuate the flavours of the melon, I leave it to
marinate in its own juices overnight, stored in little
vacuum bags. Of course I've got an extremely fancy,
and very expensive machine for this, but you can easily
get a similar effect by using ordinary freezer bags.
Do not put too much melon into each bag; suck as
much air out of the bag as you possibly can, and make
a quick tight knot. Refrigerate overnight – and then
taste the difference the following day. It simply tastes
more of melon than just melon. Just like everything
else in Miami it's never quite the way it seems, a little
enhanced… *plastic fantastic !*

FOR FOUR

**500 g large fresh octopus, calamari or squid – large pulpo squid
    needs to be simmered for 10 minutes, and cooled in iced
    water. Smaller need almost no cooking at all – 2-3 minutes**
**1 melon – water, honey, galia or cantaloupe, vacuumed if
    possible**
Chilli, finely chopped
Lime juice
Fresh coriander
Toasted sesame oil
Sea salt

Slice the chilled octopus, and together with the melon – marinate
before serving with the chilli, lime juice, coriander and sesame oil to
taste. Season with sea salt.

Melon & octopus.
Plastic fantastic

039

Milan

I was in Milan with Christian, my most-trusted head chef. Tip-top chefs from the world over had flown in to participate in Paulo Marchi's fantastical food festival '*Identita Golose*'. With the host nation standing proud, Carlo Cracco and the other chefs of Italian super-league gastronomy set to impress the stage. For me though, the highlight of the festival had to be the Victorian circus-like presentation by young Mr. Blumenthal, the now-infamous deconstruction of the classic English egg and bacon, to ice cream in a matter of seconds. The culinary Mad-Hatter of Bray is an alchemist, a magician, an entertainer. From the Italian camp things were a little simpler. They steamed, roasted and baked. Their dishes were sprinkled with a little mature Parmesan and drizzled with the finest olive oil. Most laid back indeed, like the vast majority of all good things Italian.

Gracing a table at Ristorante Cracco we had everything from wild asparagus with fresh truffles, to the most wonderful risotto with saffron and beef marrow mixed with a-half-ton of superb butter. Mini-cannelloni were filled with chocolate and nougat and served floating within a pool of dark ale. With coffee, things went a *little Heston* – small contact lenses, *yes* contact lenses made from sugared espresso were placed before us. Tempted to poke them into my eye-sockets, I luckily resisted.

Most of Milan's eateries use simplicity as the key to a good meal – sparklingly fresh fish is just brushed with beautiful olive oil and grilled over hot coals, served with lemon and a small salad. Steaks are just seared and served with melted butter and rosemary. Small delicious pasta dishes with fresh anchovies and capers, are sprinkled with a little chopped parsley, Parmesan and a hint of chilli. As in Scorsese's first *Godfather*, where the young Michael Corleone is taught to prepare pasta, as pasta should be prepared: Roast a fist of fresh garlic gently in olive oil, add tomato and white wine, leave to simmer – surrounded with love and respect. 'Someday you might have to make this for twenty men', says one of his father's henchmen, lovingly pinching young Michael's cheek.

For me the future of gastronomy lies in the past, the clean family-based creations with clear histories – not with imposingly complicated, culinary constructions and the so-called molecular deconstructions. Respect for Mother Nature's raw materials and the careful, thoughtful, respectful methods of preparation, bringing us back to the good old days, back to times where everything was a little slower, a few degrees more relaxed... when *less indeed was more*.

I wrote this recipe whilst at my summerhouse on the tiny Danish island of Sejerø. It is not Sicily, but it's still a very long way away from the busy working day. On Sejerø I have no internet, and hardly any mobile telephone connection, wonderful it is. The food we cook couldn't be simpler, clean and to-the-point, it tastes of Sejerø. It reminds me of Italy and the Italian kitchen... vine ripe tomatoes stewed gently with a little olive oil served alongside parsley-stuffed, butter-roasted horn fish. Everything is unspoilt, and life is beautiful. The dish below takes as long to prepare, as it takes the pasta to cook.

FOR FOUR

400 g good quality spaghetti or linguine
8 large fresh scallops
2 cloves garlic, finely sliced
12 courgette flowers
100 g butter cut into cubes
Lemon juice
Sea salt and black pepper
Fresh Parmesan
A little extra butter and olive oil

Bring a large saucepan of salted water to the boil for the pasta. When boiled, add the spaghetti. Stir and boil al dente.

In the meantime pan-roast the fresh scallops, golden brown in a little olive oil and a touch of butter, flavouring with the sliced garlic at the end. Give them about one minute on each side according to size. Keep warm reserving all juices. Steam the courgette flowers in a little salted water with a couple of cubes of butter.

Pour away almost all the water from the pasta, holding a cup back for the sauce. Add butter cubes and melt throughout the spaghetti, add the scallops and the pan juices. Season with lemon juice, sea salt and pepper, fresh grated Parmesan, a good glug of olive oil and serve with the steamed courgette flowers.

Scallops Corleone. *Less is indeed more*

040

Sitting, café'ed, in the most beautiful morning sunshine, a market square in the middle of Milan. Beautiful people everywhere, drinking their mid-morning espresso whilst reading the local rag. They get up and leave, and more arrive, a constant flow of chiselled, perfect people. A buzzing, zigzag of smart, shiny scooters almost makes me feel that I am an extra in a Fellini film, sipping espresso with sweet Sophia Loren or maybe the natural beauty that is the adorable Monica Bellucci..... sorry, got a little carried away there – the espresso, add a scoop of vanilla ice cream and the sunny piazza break is suddenly not just *bello*, but *bellissimo*!

Affogato al caffé

041

MY VANILLA ICE CREAM
3 vanilla pods
½ litre whipping cream
½ litre milk
180 g cane sugar
20 large pasteurised egg yolks
Zest of ½ lemon

Scrape the seeds from the vanilla pods. Roughly chop the pods. Then put both pods and seeds in the cream and milk, warm it, whilst whisking to just below boiling point. Whisk sugar and yolks to a light and airy mixture. Pour the hot cream/milk into the sugar/egg yolk mixture while continuing to whisk fiercely. Put everything back into the saucepan and leave on a low heat while continuing to stir constantly until the cream thickens. About five to seven minutes should do the trick. Add finely grated zest of lemon and leave the cream to cool completely. Pass through a sieve and place in an ice-cream machine.

Bob a little ball of ice cream into a well made espresso.

Probably the most expensive fish & 'chip' in the world. A little appetizer inspired by my trip to Bruno's caviar farm near Milan, caviar poised upon crisp duck fat fried chips... me like.

2 very large floury potatoes – King Edwards or Maris Piper maybe
500 g duck fat
8 tsp caviar

Slice the potatoes to 1.5cm x 1.5cm x 5cm. I know it sounds a little anal, but the chips will be a whole lot better if they are cut correctly and receive the correct cooking time. In a small bowl let them soak under cold running water for 10 minutes. Put the rinsed potatoes into a small saucepan and cover with fresh water, bring them to a gentle boil and salt the water, simmer carefully until almost tender. Carefully lift the potatoes from the water, drain well and place on a tray. Cover and chill for a minimum of three hours and if possible, overnight.

Pull out your trusty thermometer...

To cook, warm the duck fat to 125°C and fry the chips in it for five minutes, not colouring them too much, just a light golden. Drain them well and increase the duck fat temperature to 185°C. Fry the chip a dark golden brown – six or seven minutes.

Serve most delightfully and generously with caviar – lumpfish roe or poached, seasoned cod and turbot roe is also real good.

Fish & chip

042

Limone olive pesche verdi, chilli ripieni, cardo marinato – *Spumate Rocche Manzoni.*

Lemon' ed olives & peaches verte. Marinated chilli & cardoom, **Chicken el caviare.**

Ostriche con lime e ginger – Oyster with ginger & lime.

Scampi de Læsø, cipollini mela verde – *Langoustine from Læsø, spring oni...*

2005 San Pietro. Vigne Di San Pietro

Verdure, Astice, Caviale – *Escabeche of vegetables,* **Scottish lobster** *& caviare from Calvisius.*

Granchio Islandese, melone & menta – *Islandic crab, melon & mint leaf.*

2007 Pietranera. Marco De Bartoli

Merluzzo al vapore di acqu... zucchini & pomodoro – *Cod, fresh... courgette, rosemary.*

Rombo, cipolle, vi... – *Roasted turbot, with braised onion &... Sorrel leaf.*

2005 Villa... ...ortoletti

...funghi, faraon... *...braised guinea...*

2003

Agnello Sardini... pep peporone – ...inia, chic... red pimento.

199...

Cindhiale, pappardel... salvia – *Wild... ...delle & fresh... ...uffle. Sage leaf.*

2001 Villa Fidalma Rosso. Sportoletti

Gorgonzola, ra... *...al Forno Romano.*

Limoncello ice cream – syrup of wild str... ...rry – *Acqua... i Cedro, Blo. Nardini.*

Finocchio, cioccolato bianco, olio olive & Spezie, cioccolato amaro.

1998 Vin Santo. Il Palazzino

Rosemary financier, chocolate caramel – **Scharffen Berger.** Pistachio nou... t & white chocolate sesame.

'An evening together with Era Ora & Acquamarina' – Saturday the 2... of August, Summer 2008.

– with warmest regards & respect, you lovely people, Paul.

Rolling out of Bruno's Calvicius caviar factory, my pal Rossini and I were gasping for a chilled glass.
This little number cries out for Champagne made from pure Chardonnay. The lightly salted small slices of fresh sturgeon lie upon a little puree of milk-poached celeriac, and within a fresh vinaigrette enriched with the beast's own roe... *caviar to be precise.*

FOR FOUR

100 g superbly fresh filleted sturgeon
Sea salt
Caviar vinaigrette (see below)
1 portion of celeriac puree

Sea salt the fillet lightly, cover and marinate for about 45 minutes. Cut the fish into paper-thin slices and arrange in small bowls over a little mound of the slightly warmed celeriac puree. Finish with the caviar vinaigrette.

CELERIAC PUREE
¼ celeriac, peeled and cut into cubes
500 ml milk
Sea salt
Freshly squeezed lemon juice
1 large tbsp butter

Poach the celeriac to most tender in warmed milk. Blend to a fine puree with the butter. Adjust the consistency with a little of the celeriac milk. Season with a little sea salt and lemon juice. Keep the puree just warm, but it must under no circumstances boil.

CAVIAR VINAIGRETTE
1 tbsp finely chopped shallot
4 tbsp very finely chopped, peeled cucumber
4 tbsp olive oil
1 tbsp freshly squeezed lemon juice
2 tbsp finely chopped chives
4 generous tsp Calvisius caviar
Sea salt

Mix all the ingredients carefully. Finally mix with chives and caviar and season to taste with a little sea salt. Serve immediately over the sturgeon and celeriac puree.

Sturgeon within sturgeon

043

Wild boar, lemon & sage

044

In the mountains around Milan the wild boar roam, the lemon tree grows and wild sage seems to be everywhere – three companions that swing so well. Lemon keeps the richness of the boar in check, the sage adding its wild, earthy punch, perfuming perfectly.

FOR FOUR-SIX
1 breast of wild boar about 2.5 kg – ribs intact
Sea salt and freshly grated black pepper
6 Italian lemons – organic and unsprayed
1 large bunch fresh sage
Great olive oil

Score the breast and rub it well with sea salt and fresh cracked pepper. Rinse four of the lemons and cut them into slices. Marinate the wild boar breast overnight with the lemon slices, half a bunch of sage and 100 ml olive oil.

Ignite your grill and when the coals are ready, push them to one side so that the boar can be grilled very slowly, gently using the indirect heat from the white hot coals. Throw in a little split log or two of dry oak, or maybe woodland pine for extra flavour – it gives also a hint of smoke.

Grill the boar for about one hour, until tender. Cut the remaining two lemons in half and grill them, giving a caramelised lemon juice effect.

Serve the meat with the juice from the grilled lemons, a little fresh olive oil, sea salt and pepper. Add the remaining sage leaves, rinsed and chopped.

Korsør

'Korsør?' Why Korsør?' – That is probably the most frequent question I have been asked since moving here to this little Danish harbour town. We live a stone's throw from beach, a hop-and-a-skip from the harbour and a little pushbike ride from the forest – Korsør is quite lovely.

Our forest – a couple of completely unspoilt hectares, falling softly down to the beach. We have spent many Sundays in the forest, grilled with friends, picked mushrooms, wild herbs and flowers – sweet woodruff, chervil, ramsons and ceps, if I'm lucky – my own little wild larder.

Ramsons – never have I seen so many growing so tight – a thick racing-green carpet covering the forest floor, every year signalling the spring. The scent alone and I'm sold.

(My) centre of the universe

EKKO

The garlicky ramsons also mark the start of my new season at the restaurant. We'd fling open our doors mid-April just as the ramsons are in full bloom, so it goes without saying that they play an important role in our first menus. Langoustines swimming in a juice of green apples and ramsons, my mate Dave's spring lamb with ramsons and beach herbs, a little salted lumpfish roe to finish. Lobster wrapped in a velvety soft ramson cream – at once seductive, heavenly and most comforting.

Later in the season when the leaves are thicker and a tad more masculine in flavour, they are sautéed (as spinach) and served with veal sweetbreads or brill, maybe Dover sole fillets roasted in browned butter – or as a garnish with roast beef (large foreribs or aged cote cuts). If you sauté ramsons in plenty of butter, blend them, whisk and cool, you'll have a perfect alternative to the ordinary garlic butter.

At the end of the season we pickle the ramson buds, the process resulting in a caper-like garnish, a touch stronger, spicy in flavour. They are picked, washed and salted overnight, then marinated in a sugar-vinegar solution for a minimum of two weeks. With lamb, fallow deer, roast chicken – or ramson capers over buttered plaice, strewn over fish and chips for a change maybe?

Grilled steak with wild onions

045

Ask your local butcher boy to get cutting, with his biggest chopper in hand. The cut doesn't really matter, rib eye is delightful with its fine fat marbling, big rumps and sirloins grill wonderfully. Chateaubriand for three or four, lean almost fat-free tournedos. I used to save the very tips of butchered beef fillets for staff steaks, the fat ends are most brilliant for peppered steak au poivre. Try burgers too with this wild onion-garlicky-ramson topping, mince the beef and form it into rather long burgers, grilled with a ramson-buttered baguette – *superb*!

Find a suitable spot, far out in the woods and set up your grill – I've just been messing about with my *Big Green Egg,* porcelain grill – *my Bentley-BBQ*. Mash half, or a whole packet of butter (depending on how many you are) with finely chopped ramsons, sea salt and lemon juice. When the grill is ready and the coals and embers are glowing, season the steaks well with sea salt and grill them to a perfect medium rare – rest and smother with the ramson-butter.

It's not completely necessary to grill the steaks in the forest, but believe me, it dots the eye so well!

A childhood memory from England's sunny south coast, where I holidayed with my parents and my sister Sally. I remember playing at the water's edge, and when the tide retreated my highpoint became the small rockpools full of creepy crawlies, they entertained me for hours. Tiny beach crabs, bobbing shrimps, cockles and blue mussels; a multi-coloured palate of seaweed and ocean herbs dancing in the sun. But it was much later in life before I realised that I could actually, *eat that very rockpool.*

So far I have not managed to recreate the same rockpool dish twice – so please use this text as more of an idea, an inspiration rather than a definite recipe... maybe it'll jog a few sunny, summertime, seaside memories of your own?

MY SHOPPING LIST, A THOUGHT DANOIS...
A few local oysters – Danish from Limfjørd are delightful
Fjørd shrimps... tiny, live if poss...
Læsø langoustine, caught in the deep waters of the Kattegat
Our beautiful hummer, black lobsters
Blue 'lined' mussels
Razors of the Skagen sands
A little local mineral water
Apple vinegar from the orchards Lilleø
Unfiltered olive oil of Arbequina olives, or maybe rapeseed from Bornholm fields
Caviar by my pal Rossini
Pickled green elderberries
Beautiful cream by Grambogaard farm dairy

Steam the lobster in a touch of mineral water for three minutes. Remove the flesh from the shell, saving ALL of the precious juices, cool within the juice. Steam the cleaned mussels in a little of the lobster juice. Remove from their shells and cool again within the juices. Poach the razors and cockles and again cool in the same manor. Open the oysters, again saving the juice. Peel the shrimps and slice the shelled langoustines.

Gently lift the prepared shellfish from the intense liquid, slice and place into glass bowls. Take all of the juices from the processes, mix them with the oyster juices and pass them through a clean fine muslin to remove any impurities. Season the juices with a touch of apple vinegar or lemon, pour carefully into the bowls just covering the shellfish. Dot with a little caviar, pickled elderberries, a little olive oil and fresh cold cream, samphire and beach herbs.

PICKLED GREEN ELDERBERRIES
500 g green elderberries
100 g sea salt
500 ml apple vinegar
500 g sugar

Thoroughly pick and wash the elderberries, stir them with the salt and leave overnight. Then quickly rinse off the salt. Warm the vinegar in a saucepan to dissolve the sugar. Place the elderberries into a superbly clean jam jar, preferably scalded in boiling water. Pour over the sugared vinegar, cover and cool.

Stored well and used with a clean spoon, they'll only get better with age – *just like me.*

A rockpool of my childhood

046

BACALLA
D'IMPORTACIO
Carme Gomà

El Bulli

Barcelona

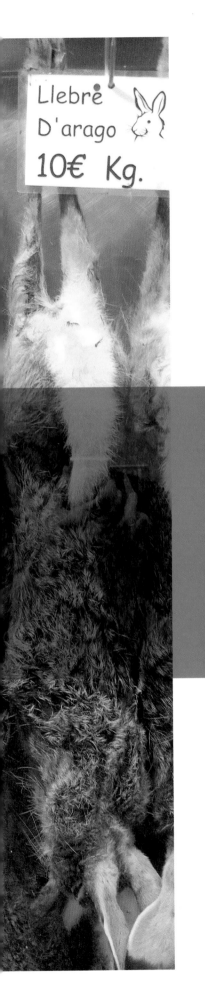

Llebre
D'arago
10€ Kg.

Barcelona is my place of refuge. Reminding me much of Copenhagen, with its small hidden side streets and forgotten alleyways, its maritime lifestyle and creative coffee drinking people.... *or would that be Cava*?

One of the world's absolutely best market halls is in Barcelona – La Boqueria has hundreds of stalls offering only the very best – wine merchants, bars, cafés and coffee brewers. In the very centre of the hall, the fishmongers rule, to the back right, the butchers. Fruits and vegetables at the front, the donkey and horse meat supplier at the very back – horse I've tried, but donkey? I'd rather ride one along Brighton beach on a warm late summer evening, than put my teeth into one...

The shops round the market sell kitchen equipment, pots and pans and chef's whites. My mate Angel used to have a little shop behind Café Ra, I love that shop; the most recent cookbooks from Ferran, Santi, Albert, Juan-Mari and all the latest high-tech equipment.

The obvious difference between Copenhagen and Barcelona, is naturally the lack of tapas bars in Copenhagen. First thing I do when I arrive in Barcelona is scuttle down to the old town, to my fav place numero uno – Cal Pep. It is the rule rather than the exception that one must queue all the way down the street before being allowed to enter Cal Pep. The last time I queued, Daniel (my brilliant restaurant manager) and I managed to polish off a half bottle of fantastical fino and an uncountable number of *petito* bottles of San Miguel, before being installed at the bar just in front of the two chefs, who were at full-steam to keep up with Cal's lunchtime madness.

Barca! Barca!

BCN

The owner of the wonderful Cal Pep sounds just like Darth Vader and has a very frank way with tourists. 'Eat, drink?' he shouted, and I replied 'Err, si senor', and that was it. No more was said. But okay, I hadn't come to chat, at Cal Pep you come to eat full stop.
Tiny silver fish turned in flour and fried crisp, fresh sardines from Galicia marinated in herby vinegar, ham cut thin as silk, grilled giant shrimps served with garlic mayonnaise and tiny squid, floating in a lake of ink with crisp chick peas, chilli and olive oil. The meat dishes are in a league of their own, grilled or fried in browned butter – there is no need for anything other than a sprig of wild rosemary and touch of sea salt. The local pork, the flank of a fresh Iberico, grilled over a roaring flame, the rest of the beast used for the most wonderful sausages. I love sausages, I dream about sausages, is that weird? ... Indeed, I think my next book might be about sausages.

I also dream about Cal Pep. This is my version of their fantastic *sepia estufas amb cigrons*.

FOR FOUR

400 g cleaned mini-squid, sepia, calamari
1 large onion, finely sliced
4 cloves garlic, sliced
1 large red pepper, sliced
1 red chilli, sliced
200 g pre-cooked chick peas
50 g hazelnuts
1 tsp squid ink
Brilliant olive oil
Sherry vinegar
Lemon juice
Sea salt

Roast the squid, fast and furious in a white-hot pan glazed with olive oil for no more than 30 seconds, add onion, garlic, peppers and chilli – give it another high-heated minute. Add the cooked chick peas and the hazelnuts. Remove from the heat and warm through, flavouring with the squid ink, olive oil, sherry vinegar and lemon. Correcting the seasoning at the very end with sea salt.

Good bread, and that's that.

Cal Pep
sepia estufas amb cigrons

047

Milk toffee & strawberries D:HYD

048

Barcelona was the centre of the culinary-storm that is molecular gastronomy. The Lord Ferran Adrià of El Bulli has, like no other chef, rocked the very soul of *haute cuisine Française* with his new preparation techniques and his most unusual and very original ways of gastronomic thinking. Much has been written about this man – he has the respect of a whole generation – *enough said.*

Machines for drying or dehydrating selected foods can be purchased quite cheaply today. When I acquired my first dehydrator several years ago from Australia, it cost a small fortune. In this recipe, by drying and pulverising the strawberries, the essential strawberry flavour becomes most intense, and the consistency makes the strawberry experience very, very special indeed. You can do it with all kinds of berries, and indeed fruits or vegetables. Crush the dried berries and store in a sealed container, dark, dry and cool. It'll only get better. Today you can also buy dried fruit and berry powders from specialist grocers or suppliers.

FOR THE SMALL TOFFEES
800 g sugar
100 g butter
175 g whipping cream – yes, weigh the cream for this one
1 tin condensed milk (aprox. 425 g)
2 tbsp golden syrup
2 tbsp dried strawberry powder + a little extra for sprinkling

In a saucepan, melt together the sugar, butter and cream stirring over a low heat. Add the condensed milk and bring the mixture to a gentle boil for five minutes, again stirring constantly. Remove the saucepan from the heat and stir in well the golden syrup and powdered strawberry.

Pour the mixture into a square tray, or container, so you can cut it into small toffees afterwards. Cool the mixture in the tray overnight. Cut the toffees into small cubes and roll in the strawberry powder before serving with coffee.

Jamón ibérico,
sardines &
raspberries

049

You can hardly call this a recipe; a combination of flavours would be more astute. An unusual, but still completely logical flavour code, on which I base most of my dishes: add salt to a bitter element, combine with acid and sweet and the result is the now so familiar umami. Here when I combine the well-hung salted ham from the Iberian black-footed pigs which roam the forests of Extremadura in Spain and southern Portugal, having the characteristically bitter, earthy and herby notes, with the spicy acidic tones from the vinegar-pickled Galician sardines, the flavour combinations lift. The raspberries give a sweet, fruit caramel kind of balance that I am most fond of.

This three-taste combo, I've used for years now. The guises have changed but the basic equation has stayed the same.

THIS IS HOW

Ibérico with sardines and fresh raspberries, over crisp sourdough.

Raspberry jelly with sardines wrapped in Ibérico.

Ibérico gel, sardine consommé and raspberry vinegar pearl.

Pizzetta of Ibérico and sardine puree, dried raspberry powder.

Ibérico, sardine tempura, raspberry puree.

Sardine-raspberry salad with dried Ibérico.

Sardine ravioli, Ibérico, raspberry vinaigrette.

Raspberry vinagre sorbetto, Iberico-sardine salad.

Ibérico crostini with sardine-raspberry-oil.

So on, and so on....

In Gaudi's Barcelona every meal starts with *pan con tomate* at no matter which restaurant or tapas bar, and no matter at what meal... here you'd have good bread and beautiful butter. Thick slices of grilled bread, rubbed with a little garlic, lots of lovely olive oil and fresh grated tomatoes. In genuine Gaudi-fashion I have altered the concept a little, twisted it if you like. I grill the bread with a little honey, caramelise the tomatoes and season the ice cream with olive oil and *voila*!

FOR FOUR

OLIVE OIL ICE CREAM
250 ml milk
75 g sugar
3 egg yolks
125 g crème fraîche 38%
500 ml super quality olive oil
Juice from ½ lemon

CARAMELISED TOMATO
A tray of cherry tomatoes on the vine
A little cane sugar
A little sea salt and black pepper
Olive oil
Sherry vinegar

4 thick slices of sourdough bread
Honey or maple syrup

Both ice cream and tomatoes should be made in advance.

Bring the milk to just under boiling point, whisking and dissolving the sugar. Pour the mixture over the whisked egg yolks, whisking continuously whilst you pour. The mixture will thicken slightly, add the crème fraiche and the olive oil – pour the mixture into a blender and blend for one minute. Cool slightly and run in an ice-cream machine, adding the lemon juice. Freeze until needed.

Wash and halve the tomatoes. Place them on a baking tray lined with baking paper, tomato seeds side up. Season with a little sugar, salt and pepper, olive oil and sherry vinegar. Bake the tomatoes overnight at 50°C/gas ⅛.

The following day, place the tomatoes into a clean and scalded jam jar, pour the marinade over and refrigerate for at least two days if possible.

Drizzle the bread well with olive oil, honey or maple syrup, bake golden and crisp. Serve the tempered tomatoes on the sweet caramelised toast with a large spoonful of olive oil ice cream, and drip with a little of the tomato marinade from the jar.

Pan con tomate & olive oil ice cream

050

I came to Denmark back in 1994. After a stint as gardener/tennis court-looker-after'er at the local tennis club I landed a position at Søllerød Kro, an ex-starred traditional inn with one of Denmark's most expensive addresses.

I had prepared a Danish classic a few nights before with the mother-in-law, koldskål – a chilled dessert soup of whisked buttermilk, thickened with egg yolks, sweetened with sugar and zinged up with lots of lemon. Small biscuits are crushed over the dish at the end... we prepared it at the restaurant for staff dinner, and it got us thinking.

Taking the basic ingredients from this simple, cool summer soup we tried to do something a little different for the evening guests – we transformed them into mousses, foams, jellies, cakes, ice cream, terrines and soufflés. The mother-in-law's buttermilk soup had now been deconstructed – and constructed again.

Gastronomic evolution is most important, we need to push on, without however, forgetting to show respect for the classics. These classics were indeed once regarded as new wave – the passing on of these age-old taste combinations is imperative for the training of our next generation. Strawberries and cream, orange and dark chocolate, vanilla and rhubarb – cheese and pickle maybe, even eggs and bacon. The latter being the most English of English, another classic combination that was, a few years ago, flavour and texture deconstructed and remade in dessert form by that young scallywag Blumenthal, lovely bloke he is.

My version of café con leche is also a little different. It's a make-up of the coffee's original construction, still using the same base products, with a twist'ette – a spoon of lightly salted rich toffee ice cream, crisp caramelised white chocolate, finely chopped chocolate beans and roasted grated coffee beans. Topped with the lightest vanilla milk mousse, fine grated chocolate and coffee beans, finishing off with a welcome drizzle of warm espresso syrup.

... a sofa, if you please!

144

FOR SIX OR EIGHT

CARAMELISED WHITE CHOCOLATE
400 g white chocolate

Melt the chocolate and pour onto a silicone mat. Bake the chocolate until well browned at 180°C/gas 4 for 10 to 15 minutes. Leave to cool completely, before you break it into small pieces.

ICE CREAM
600 ml condensed milk
400 ml whipping cream
2 tbsp honey
12 egg yolks

Bring the condensed milk, cream and honey to just under boiling point. Pour over the well whisked yolks, whisking constantly. Place back onto a gentle heat and stir until the mix thickens. Leave to cool, and run in an ice machine. Freeze until needed.

MILK MOUSSE
400 ml full cream milk
25 g sugar
1 split vanilla pod
3 small leaves of gelatine, softened in cold water
2 egg whites

Pour the milk, sugar and vanilla into a saucepan and gently warm it through, so as the sugar dissolves the vanilla infuses. Whisk in the softened gelatine. Leave the mixture to cool completely. When cooled whisk in the egg whites and pour the vanilla milk into a siphon bottle with two canisters of gas, and shake well. Chill.

ESPRESSO SYRUP
3 double espressos
3 tbsp brown sugar

Boil the espressos together with the sugar to a thick, sticky syrup. Keep warm.

TO SERVE
Chopped coco nibs
Grated coffee beans

... arrange as you see fit.

Café con leche
Paul's way

051

Summer

The gastronomic melting pot

Simmering, steaming, bubbling – London boils over with cuisines from every corner of the globe, and all of the seven seas.

The city's collection of culinary traditions have been brought together, nurtured and nourished over the past hundreds of years. Throughout the times colonies have been won, lost, taken over and most humbly given back. All though have luckily made their impression on the great city, and upon London's gastronomic culture.

To the east of London is a street which is completely and totally unlike any other street I have been to. Green Street, E7 in Newham is a tiny taste of beautiful India, everyone and everything is Indian – apart from pale old me.

As a boy I occasionally drove up to the East End, at weekends with my Mum and Dad, in his shiny polished, lobster red Austin Maxi, later in the chocolate brown Austin Princess – *a taste for cars, my Dad didn't really have*. The shortest route by car brought us past the infamous Essex nightclub, The Circus Tavern. It was here that the girls of *Page 3* hung out, in their undersized outfits stuffed with their oversized chests, and their just as *oversized-Capri-driving-gangster-boyfriends*. Passing the Ford factory in Dagenham, shortly after came Upton Park the home of West Ham United (and the home of real football). A genuine full-blown football fan I have probably never been but, here's something about West Ham. I can remember eating dodgy grilled burgers and hotdogs with my uncle outside the stadium – they didn't really taste that wonderful, but the smell of those fried onions – go hand in hand with the unforgettable experience it was to see Trevor Brooking score yet another incredible goal against the arch enemies from Arsenal, Spurs or Millwall.

Green Street is just around the corner from Upton Park – the street is full to bursting point with authentic Asian restaurants with food from the north, south, east and west, Kashmir, Bangladesh, Bengal, the Punjab and Pakistan. Every corner of Indian cuisine is colourfully represented in Green Street. You are drawn by the aromas of simmering vindaloo, and bubbling, strongly spiced daal. Crisp samosas filled with coriander, mint and fresh peas. Dark roasted onions and garlic bound within a bread dough for a tandoori naan. The air is thick with cumin, cardamom, coriander, cinnamon. Sacks are full of colourful spices, ground chilli, yellow mustard seeds, golden turmeric and the most beautiful silk saris hang from every street corner. Then there are the people of Little India, most happy, most positive, optimistic and full of life. I long to return with the next generation soon.

FOR EIGHT

1.5 kg neck of lamb, cut into large cubes
8 large onions, sliced
16 cloves garlic
4 tbsp freshly chopped ginger
4 red peppers, grilled, skin removed and chopped
4 large tomatoes, cubed
2 tbsp paprika
2 tsp smoked paprika
1 tbsp garam masala
1 tbsp turmeric
1 tsp sea salt
4 tbsp tomato puree
2 red chillies, seeds removed and chopped
2 bunches coriander
2 tsp cumin seeds, toasted and crushed
2 tsp coriander seeds, toasted and crushed
1 tsp black pepper, toasted and crushed
Ghee

Mix all the ingredients in a large bowl, cover and leave to marinate, refrigerated overnight. Remove the lamb, leaving the marinade behind, and brown it in a very hot pan with a spoonful or two of hot ghee. Put everything into a large saucepan and cover with fresh cold water. Leave to simmer at low heat for four hours, or place covered into an oven at 150°C/gas 2.

Reduced, thick, intense and rich – serve with fresh okra fried in a little browned butter with lime and green chilli, fresh mango, cut and caramelised with sugar, rice wine vinegar, fennel seeds and red chilli. Salted cucumber salad with red onions, coriander and mint leaves. Classic Indian raita made with grated, salted cucumber mixed with yoghurt, lemon zest and chopped mint. Cauliflower fried in butter with crushed cumin seeds, green chilli and zest of lime. Potato-pea samosa, *my own onion bhaji,* crisp pappadums and grilled naans. Not forgetting my favourite lime pickle bought from Mr. Patel's spice shop on Green St. ... as strong as a horse!

Neck of lamb 'Rogan josh'

052

During the years 1892-93, when the Australian Grand Opera singer Dame Nellie Melba wasn't singing in the Covent Garden Opera House, she was eating within the grand dining rooms at The Strand's Savoy Hotel. The only thing to outshine the great diva's ego, was her appetite, and this in turn was seduced and satisfied by none other than the great chef Mon. Auguste Escoffier.

It was particularly the desserts that Dame Nellie found most appealing. In those days the sweet wonders were arranged on large polished, flowered trolleys, wheeled in by the waiters with starched collars, penguin jackets and shiny shoes – they were the stars of the show back-in-the-day, chefs were mere mortals.

One summer Savoy evening Auguste Escoffier threw together a dessert for the young lady – and today it's one of cuisine's great classics. He poached a few peaches in lightly sugared water, peeled them and served them with vanilla ice cream, poised within a pool of pureed fresh raspberries *et voila*, Pêche Melba was born.

These days Escoffier's basic recipes form the corner stone of every professional chef's recipe repertoire. Pêche Melba is also at the base of this following recipe where the challenge was to find an acidic, fresh and sweet contrast to the richness of the foie gras. Summer peaches add sweetness and bite, the raspberries add acid and these two basic elements are rounded off with a sweet and sour vanilla syrup *gastrique*.

Homage to Auguste
Escoffier 1846-1935.
The king of chefs,
and chef of kings.

FOR FOUR FOIE GRAS FANS

4 slices of foie gras 'au torchon' (see below)
Peaches
Raspberries
Raspberry puree spiked with raspberry vinegar
Macadamia nuts
Woodland sorrel leaves
Fresh tarragon leaves
Vanilla gastrique (see below)
Olive oil

FOIE GRAS 'AU TORCHON'
200 g fresh foie gras
4 g fine sea salt
1 tbsp of sweet white wine
1 tbsp of brandy

Temper, trim and remove all blood pockets and sinew from the fresh foie gras, place into an ovenproof dish dressed with the sea salt, sweet white wine and brandy for two hours. Bake at 110°C/gas ¼ for 5 minutes, leave to cool. Carefully lift the liver from the fat, draining well, roll it in a cloth or cling film. If you are using a cloth, press it carefully so the excess fat runs out – if using cling film, make a few holes with a needle and gently roll to remove the excess fat. Refrigerate, leaving overnight if possible, the flavour will only improve.

VANILLA GASTRIQUE
100 ml Champagne vinegar
100 g light cane sugar
1 split vanilla pod

Boil the three ingredients to a thick syrup, the recipe given yields far too much, it stores well refrigerated.

Arrange the sliced foie gras with thin slices of raw, ripe peach, raspberries, toasted macadamia nuts, a little woodland sorrel and tarragon leaves. Dress with a little raspberry vinegar spiked with raspberry puree, vanilla *gastrique*, and a couple of drops of olive oil. Dress the foie gras with a little sea salt.

Foie gras 'au torchon' & pêche, Dame Nellie Melba

053

Every time I put a leg of lamb in the oven on a spring Sunday, I think of my nan, it brings a tear to my eye. My nan's lamb was set at a low temperature, and slow-roasted forever. It was put in the oven first thing in the morning, and was basted constantly whilst roasting. Three different types of potatoes were always served, potatoes roasted in the fat of the lamb, boiled potatoes and mashed potatoes with lots of butter. The latter was primarily for grandad, all the vegetables we had came from his garden – or rather his gardens. My grandad also looked after the neighbours' gardens – I can still see him there, garden fork in hand, sweating in the late afternoon sun, wearing big old muddy Wellington boots, braces and an off-white, well-ironed, long sleeved shirt buttoned from his navel to his cuff. My dear grandad had war tattoos, he only ever rolled up his sleeves when he entered the house to see the horse racing from Newmarket or to have a well-earned slice of homemade Victoria sponge.

FOUR OR SIX

1 fresh leg of lamb, around 2 kg
Butter
Sea salt
Flour

Turn on the oven to 170°C/gas 3½. Trim the leg of lamb and rub it with butter and sea salt. Sprinkle a little flour over it, this helps to make the fat crisp. Roast the lamb for two hours and let it rest well before carving. Please do remember to deglaze the roasting tin for lamb juices, the gravy will be most splendid indeed.

MINT SAUCE
1 small bunch fresh mint
100 ml malt vinegar
1 tbsp sugar

Wash and chop the mint. Mix with vinegar and sugar and leave for two hours to infuse.

Leg of lamb, minted

054

Fruit leather with aged Stilton

055

Explaining the fact in Denmark is no easy task – Stilton being not just any old blue cheese, nor is Stilton just Stilton! Stilton is the national pride of Old England. Only several dairies in England are allowed to produce Stilton, creating it from the milk of the most beautiful cows that have grazed the fields in Lancashire, Nottinghamshire and Derbyshire. Funnily enough, the town Stilton, which has given its name to the cheese, is in fact in Cambridgeshire, and Stilton has never been produced at a dairy within the town of Stilton… *now there's a fact for you.*

The Victorian preserving method of 'fruit leather' creates a semi-dried, elastic, sweet and sour chutney. The fruit is boiled with the sugar and then left to dry for a couple of days, until it is leathery and lovely! For this recipe I have used plums, but you can use any kind of fruit: apples, pears, berries, grapes. Just remember to experiment with the taste, since the amount of sugar needed depends on the type of fruit or berry you use, and of course the time of year. *The later the summer day, the sweeter the fruit.*

PLUM'ED FRUIT LEATHER
1 kg plums
200 g sugar
500 ml water
Stilton, the best you can find – I adore a well-aged Colston Bassett, made within the Vale of Belvoir.

Wash the plums and remove the stones. Put the plums, sugar and water into a saucepan and leave to simmer on low heat for about two hours. Pass the thick compote through a fine mesh sieve. Spread over silicone mats, it should be about 3mm thick. Place the mats in the oven at 50°C/gas ⅛ and leave overnight.

When the mixture is semi-dry and leathery, it can be cut with a warm knife and put in a plastic box with layers of baking paper between each layer of fruit leather.

Serve with Stilton and a good, crusty loaf, in the garden with a glass of IPA.

Without doubt the great Marco Pierre White has indirectly been the one chef who has had the biggest influence on my professional career.

One day, many moons ago whilst skiving from college, I was dozing upon my parents' sofa clicking at the TV remote. Suddenly Marco appeared on the screen – a Jim Morrison-like apparition, dressed in a ragatty chef's jacket, clad with a worn blue and white striped butcher's apron. Making the most wonderful dishes in a chaos of classical music, sweat, tears – whisking in the odd four-letter-word for good measure.

I saw my future that day, and to this day, the blue and white colours still hang around my neck – I always thought it was a shame that they weren't claret and blue.

This is his lemon tart which I have made proudly for several decades now... a proper chef's dessert it is too.

Tarte au citron Marco's way

056

FOR EIGHT

PASTRY
500 g flour
175 g icing sugar
250 g unsalted butter (room temperature)
Zest of 1 organic lemon
Seeds from 1 vanilla pod
1 ½ large eggs whisked

LEMON CREAM
9 eggs
400 g sugar
Zest of 2 organic lemons
Juice from 5 lemons
250 ml double cream

Sugar for glazing

Quickly mix all the ingredients for the pastry into a dough, using a food processor if possible. Wrap the dough in film and leave in the fridge for at least two hours. Roll the pastry out to about 2-3mm and place it in a buttered tart ring upon a papered baking tray, the ring measuring 4cm high and 20cm diameter. Place in the fridge for a further half hour. Cover the pastry case with baking paper and fill with baking beans, bake in a hot oven at 180°C/gas 4 for ten minutes. Remove the pastry from the oven, remove the beans and the baking paper, baking the pastry case blind for a further ten minutes, afterwards turn the oven down to 120°C/gas ½.

Whisk the eggs, sugar and lemon zest until light and airy and add lemon juice. Whisk in the cream. Remove any foam from the top of the mixture before pouring into the warm pastry case. Bake the tart for a further 30 minutes at 120°C/gas ½ and leave to rest for one hour. *Do not chill the tart – lemon tarts aren't refrigerated, they are eaten on command*!!

Glaze the tart with sugar using a small blowtorch or a fantastically hot grill.

Comwall

Well, I believe my culinary interest takes its starting point in a single love affair with food. Not Michelin-star food, just food.

I was a small, rather round and happy boy with a very healthy appetite and a passion for anything edible. My mum's oven-baked onion soup is still a big favourite and my nan's Sunday lunch could not have been better, slow cooked topside of beef with three or four kinds of vegetables from my grandad's garden and lots of gravy (*skysovs* to you Danes). And always three kinds of potato – mashed, boiled and roasted in dripping. A sweet baked rice pudding was placed on the table in a large bowl for dessert. We each took a portion and my beloved grandad always had the rest from the bowl afterwards, he loved the sugary skin of the milk. Funny that milk-skin is so bloody trendy now.

A Cornish summer 2007, part 1

During the summer holidays, my little sister Sally and I squeezed into my dad's beautiful old VW camper van, pure white with a large highly-polished VW logo at the front and inside there was a kitchen, beds for me and Sally, my mum and dad, fridge, and a tailor-made awning, it was tops! *I'd give my right arm for that van now.* We munched our way through seaside town after seaside town – along the English coastline through darkest Dorset, wonderful Devon and my beloved Cornwall. Summer life was just one giant Cornish pasty with an extra serving of clotted cream on the side. We explored every rockpool, beach, bay and harbour with my folks back in those days, stopping only to taste the wares of the local fishermen, bakers and butchers… wonderful!

My Old Man loved the many small farm shops and the country roads' gastronomic stopping places. He bought everything from fresh warm new laid chicken eggs to homemade marmalades, bread of all kinds and the season's new vegetables. Our garage at home in Essex was a cornucopia of wonderful unspoiled farm foods. I have spent many a day with my folks picking the most wonderful strawberries near Tiptree, which today is the home of the world famous marmalades.

Recently I had a real English summer holiday with my two sons and my lovely wife, caravanning with the wife's sweet cousin Kathrine, her fab-hub Alistair and their offspring. Cornwall with the family was superb. After violent rainstorms earlier in the week we had five days with full sun and warm summer winds, perched on a hill overlooking tiny Fowey. The residents in the seaside town were as usual fantastically friendly, iced apple cider and the local foods tasted wonderful. Day after day the Cornish pasties were to sob for, and my beloved fish and chips, which I'd missed so badly, tasted just as it should – beautifully fresh fish, fried in a light and crisp beer batter, seasoned generously with sea salt and malt vinegar, large delicious fat chips alongside.

Hurry up, and make this folks, find the nearest harbour. Roll up your trousers, dip your pinkies in the water, not forgetting your knotted hankie. Chilled cider and the scene is set.

MY FISH AND CHIPS FOR FOUR

1 bottle vegetable oil
4 large'ish haddock, hake, pollock or indeed seasonal cod fillets
100 g self raising flour
1 bottle of ale – you won't need all of it sodrink the rest you may
6 large potatoes cut as chips, King Ed's or Maris Piper

Slice the potatoes to your preferred chip size, but not too small and thin. Cut them rather uniform, I know it sounds a little strange, but the chips will be a whole lot better if they are cut correctly and receive the correct cooking time. In a small bowl let them soak under cold running water for 10 minutes. Place the rinsed potatoes into a saucepan and cover with fresh water, bring them to a gentle boil and salt the water, simmer carefully until just tender. Carefully lift the potatoes from the water, drain well and place onto a tray. Cover and chill for a minimum of three hours and if possible, overnight.

Put your trust in a little thermometer...

To cook, heat the oil to 125°C and fry the chips in it for five minutes, not colouring them too much, just a light golden. Drain them well and increase the oil temperature to 185°C. Fry the chips, a dark golden brown – six or seven minutes, and keep them hot whist you cook the fish.

Mix the flour, adding the beer and salt to a thick batter. Season the fish with salt, sprinkle with a little flour. Dip in the beer batter and fry the fish in hot oil until golden and crisp. Serve seasoned well with sea salt, malt vinegar, and I like fresh ground black pepper too.

For a finer and more restaurant-like fish and chips, serve with a tartare sauce. This acidic mayonnaise-based sauce is creamy, crisp and fresh and super simple to make.

6 tbsp mayonnaise
2 tbsp chopped capers
2 tbsp chopped cornichons
2 tbsp chopped parsley
1 tbsp chopped tarragon
½ tsp black pepper
Zest and juice of 1 lemon

Mix the above and infuse for a while.

Fish & chips
- the love of my life

057

'Is gran-gran having dinner with Elvis now?' my son asked when my dad passed away. Cornish pasty was his absolute favourite dish... you can keep your Lobster Thermidors, your white truffles, your shiny caviar and your shucked oysters! My dad's way to spend his late summer afternoon in one of Cornwall's many, many harbours was to devour a freshly baked pasty, filled with lamb and delicious local vegetables, seasoned to the hilt with chopped thyme and well seasoned with salt and black pepper. A cup of tea and he was a happy little boy again.

They always work, the simple things in life. A Mr Whippy or a milky Southend Rossi ice cream on a hot summer's day, a hot sausage grilled over coal with sweet mustard and served with Sauce Heinz. Or perhaps a lovely pan-fried plaice with a salty sour cucumber salad, boiled new spuds and parsley sauce.

Simple food should adorn every family table. I often hear people ask my favourite mother-in-law whether it's not a nightmare when Paul comes for dinner. No, she replies every time. 'I don't care. He will have to eat what is served, or go hungry from the table'. I've never gone hungry from her table. Her secret spice is love, passion. Food made from the heart... it just tastes better. From my dear mother-in-law's super *frikadeller* (meat balls, to you) with creamed white cabbage, to a good old fashioned Tournedos Rossini, topped with toasted foie gras, fresh truffles and Madeira sauce.

Apart from being my dad's favourite dish, the little Cornish pasty can be traced back to the 1300's and was a delicacy which was enjoyed by the aristocracy. In those days it was filled with game, wild birds, even river salmon and trout. A story goes, that Lady Jane Seymour, the delectable young belle of great King Henry VIII loved a pasty or two. Not until the industrial revolution at the end of the nineteenth century was the Cornish pasty, named Cornish pasty, it was the ultimate convenience food of the time. The folded pastry edge meant that the pasty was a perfect lunch for manual labourers and dirty old miners – covered from head-to-toe in mud, dust and often also arsenic. They could hold the hard pastry edge without touching the pasty itself, pasty eaten and the dirty edge thrown away, job done (god I do hate the Gordon'ed phrase!). Luck was brought to the mines by the naughty Knockers who lived within the dark tunnels, most happy they were for the pasty remains left behind by the tired and homebound miners.

A Cornish summer
2007, part 2

Summer of 2007, sitting at the harbour of Clovelly with my family. My two little Vikings tasted their first Cornish pasty. I cannot describe how happy I was to see their little summer-sun'ed smiling faces, experiencing this simple typical British summer holiday which I loved so dearly as a child. Life is good!

FOR FOUR CORNWALL'ISTS

4 round bases of puff pastry (made with butter) with a diameter of approx. 25 cm

FILLING
400 g fresh lean lamb cut into small cubes – I like the rump, who doesn't?
1 onion finely diced
2 carrots finely diced
¼ swede finely diced
2 large baking potatoes finely diced
1 good tbsp freshly chopped thyme
Sea salt and freshly ground black pepper
Butter and egg yolk

Set the oven to 180°C/gas 4.

Mix the filling together and season well. Divide the filling onto the four rounds of puff pastry. Top each of the pasty fillings with a good teaspoon of butter.

Close them to half moons and brush with egg yolk. Sprinkle with salt and pepper, bake golden brown, they will need 20-30 minutes.

Serve with pickled onion or indeed Branston.

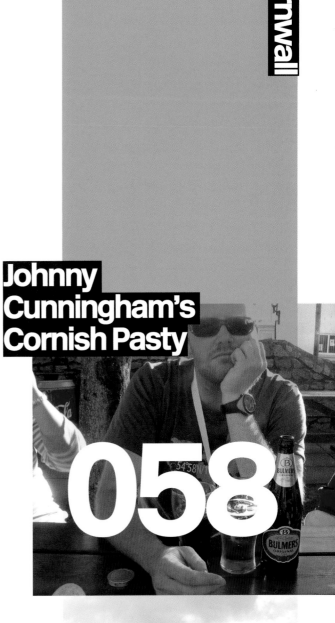

Johnny Cunningham's Cornish Pasty

058

A traditional old English summer seaside classic. My mum loves this dish, again along the harbour with a glass of cool white wine.

FOR FOUR

100 g butter
¼ tsp cayenne
¼ tsp ground nutmeg
100 g whole fresh shrimps and 400 g peeled – we use here summer Fjord shrimps or brown shrimps from the tiny Danish island of Rømø

Lemon
White asparagus
Toast

Gently melt the butter and add the whole fjord shrimps. Leave to simmering, to infuse for ten minutes. Sieve the butter carefully, pushing through as much of the shrimp juices as possible, the flavour will be incomparable. Season well the warm shrimp butter, adding the cayenne and nutmeg, fold in the peeled shrimps and finish with a touch of lemon juice.

Divide into four small glass jars, press lightly, sealing the top with a little melted butter. Refrigerate for an hour or so.

Serve with steamed asparagus, hot toast and lemon.

Potted shrimps

059

In reality this is not a typical Cornish dessert but when you make Eton Mess with the cream of Cornwall, it'll only get better. Only use the darkest and juiciest strawberries, raspberries or indeed blackberries (in this case the blackest and not the reddest!) When making my *Copenhagen Mess* I use poached rhubarb, the season's first, Queen Margrethe loves it!

The story goes that Eton Mess was first put together at Eton College, just outside Windsor. It was, and is, a quintessential summer dessert, which was originally served up for the school's gentlemen, in a small crisp meringue base filled with whipped cream and topped with fresh berries. Their trick, immediately after receiving said dessert, was to smash it into a thousand pieces before devouring, hence the name *Eton Mess*.

FOR FOUR/SIX ETONIANS

400 ml lightly whipped cream – whipping or indeed double, depending on your mood
2 handfuls lightly crushed meringue (see below)
4 handfuls fresh, ripe berries – for example strawberries, raspberries, blueberries and blackberries

MERINGUE
6 large egg whites
½ tsp fine sea salt
200 g honey heated to 120°C
1 tsp cornflour
1 tsp white wine vinegar

Using an electric whisker, whisk the egg whites until light and airy in a very clean and dry metal bowl. Add salt and continue to whisk. Pour in the warm honey, a little at a time, while continuing to whisk. Whisk until the mixture is completely cooled. Fold in cornflour and vinegar.

Spread the mixture onto silicone mats and bake it in the oven, previously set at 110°C/gas ¼, cook for 1½ hours, turn off the oven and leave to cool for 3 or 4 hours until dry and crisp. Leave the meringue to cool completely before storing in an airtight container.

Eton Mess

I don't know whether Sejerø is blessed – or whether the fact is that I am blessed because I am so lucky to know about Sejerø. The picturesque little slither of an island lies to the north-west of Sjælland and is delightfully untouched.

Sejerø is our second home… open fields, unspoilt small woodlands, deserted beaches and wonderful fresh air. You start to wind down the minute you board the ferry from the tiny harbour of Havnsø, gently sailing for just under an hour, being freed from worries and your daily chores. No appointments, no obligations. My computer grunts strangely when it arrives on Sejerø, internet access is virtually non-existent, and my mobile telephone almost laughs at the thought of me even contemplating a connection to the mainland.

My wife and I were married in the little old church on Sejerø, and held the wedding party in the garden of her folk's farm by the village pond. We were 120 at the party, which is impressive when you consider that there are only about 400 permanent residents on the island. We grilled beef and local lamb from the island, seasoned with the island's wild herbs. New baby potatoes, fennel and beetroot with lots of mayonnaise, and for dessert thousands of strawberries with oceans of fresh cream and sugar. We finished in style with an enormous heart-shaped wedding cake, feeding each other in true *Priscilla and Elvis* style.

Originally our little harbour house was used for sorting fishing nets. This was where they washed and repaired the nets from the small fishing boats which were formerly part of Sejerø's little harbour, unfortunately most of them have now gone. My wife's grandad bought the house many years ago and it has now been passed on to my wife's generation, worth more to us than its weight in gold.

If I could live there, I most certainly would – but live off Sejerø, I don't think I could.

This chapter is dedicated to all the lovely people who have willingly given of Sejerø's charm – above all our neighbours, Inge and her Helton, the indomitable fisherman, Erik and my favourite mother-in-law Kitty, Finn and Doris. *Jeg elsker Sejerø, tak.*

Sejerø blessed

EKKL

FOR FOUR

2 small fennel bulbs, sliced
2 spring onions, finely chopped
1 lemon, thinly sliced, plus a little extra lemon juice for the end
Olive oil
8 anchovies in olive oil
4 plaice, sparklingly fresh, cleaned and skinned
Sea salt and black pepper

GARNISH
Pickled ramson capers (see below)
Newly dug new potatoes
Fennel tops

Set the oven at 180°C/gas 4.

Mix the finely sliced fennel, spring onion and lemon, with olive oil and anchovies. Place in an oven-proof dish. Arrange the plaice on top, brush well with olive oil and lemon juice, season well. Cover with foil and bake for 20 minutes... removing the foil and baking further for five.

Serve with pickled ramson capers, steamed new potatoes and fennel tops.

PICKLED RAMSON CAPERS
When the ramsons have started to flower, collect the buds – 200 g buds, salted with 100 g sea salt – and leave overnight. Rinse the salt off, pickle in a warm marinade of 500 ml apple vinegar boiled with 500 g sugar. Pour into scalded jam jars and leave for a couple of weeks if possible before use.

Plaice with fennel, ramson capers & anchovies

061

When I talk about our little summer house on tiny Sejerø, I always end up saying that you have to bring most things from home, because you cannot really buy anything on the island... a little white lie. The local restaurant cooks simple local stuff and has a small selection of Hansen's brilliant ice cream for those hot summer afternoons, and out at the lighthouse there's a small farm with fantastically rich, creamy honey, and you can order veal and lamb from the island's farmers. And then there is Jesper, who owns the farm on the edge of Nordby. He has geese, and his chickens lay the best eggs you can imagine with the most deep-orange yolk, my breakfast omelettes are wonderful!

When you leave Sejerby, past the local football ground on the left, you will see an old sign displaying the wares of Karl and his sweet Ella. Their vegetables are in a class of their own... newly dug carrots and parsnips, the most intense, superbly strong horseradish roots and their tiny bulbs of fresh garlic. Shallots, courgettes, cucumbers, fennel and mountains of green summer herbs. Beetroot, salads, and tiny potatoes that taste as they should.

FOR FOUR

1 large beautiful free range chicken from Jesper's farm
Fresh herbs
Sea salt and freshly ground black pepper
Butter
Fresh vegetables from Karl and Ella – *if you are on the island that is!*

Stuff the chicken with fresh herbs, season the inside well with sea salt and fresh ground pepper. Push in the Parson's nose and truss the bird. Rub the skin generously with butter and season again well. Set the oven to 185°C/gas 4½ for one and a half hours, depending on the size of the chicken.

After an hour add the vegetables. Dress well with the chicken juices and leave to roast together with the chicken... *I tend to blanch the potatoes first in well salted water.*

Choose your own vegetables, that's up to you and your gracious greengrocer, but a good classic Danish cucumber salad is a must. Roughly peel and slice one large cucumber, salting well for about an hour, drain and pour over a pickling liquor of 200 ml apple vinegar whisked well with 100 g sugar, and throw in a split fresh chilli and a few bay leaves. Leave to infuse until needed.

Jesper's beautiful chicken, with Karl & Ella's vegetables

062

A local Sejerø recipe inspired by our lovely neighbours on the island, twisted a little. Inge makes her *fuldskager* with minced pork and onions, they taste delicious, but a while ago I heard a rumour that they were first made by using the cheap off-cuts of the local island lamb... wow!
Fuldskager are small steamed bread dumplings – a little like dim-sum.

20 SMALL *'FULDSKAGER'*
THE FILLING
500 g minced lamb
1 onion, finely chopped
1 pinch allspice
1 tbsp fresh thyme leaf
Sea salt and freshly ground black pepper

Mix the meat thoroughly with the other ingredients. Shape into 20 small balls and refrigerate.

THE DOUGH
75 g oats
200 ml warm water
A little plain flour
½ tsp fine sea salt

Soften the oats in the warm water for 10 minutes. Add flour a little at a time while stirring thoroughly. Continue until the pastry cleanly leaves the sides of the bowl. Add the fine salt and knead to a smooth dough, leave to rest for an hour.

Take a little flour in your hands and shape small thin pancakes from the dough. Wrap the lamb balls within the dough, sealing them carefully.

Simmer the *fuldskager* gently in lightly salted water for around 20 minutes, drain well and serve with a rich gravy of lamb flavoured with thyme, and perhaps a little steamed, buttered spring cabbage.

Helton & Inge's steamed 'fuldskager'

063

One of our Sejerø-family specialities, and it was one of the staff's absolute favourite dishes at the restaurant. So simple, so good! And with a few buttered new potatoes and a small green salad, you are home free. Bake the fillets whole in a dish or try to bake the fish separately, each in their own little jam jars. The herbed juices gather at the bottom, it tastes wonderful – if I could mass produce that taste, jar it and sell it... by this time next year (as Del often proclaimed), *we'd be millionaires!*

FOR FOUR

4 thick and completely fresh skinless cod fillets each 150 g
200 g butter
Sea salt
Lemon
A couple of handfuls of herbs from the garden, for example
    parsley, mint, chives, oregano, lovage, thyme, tarragon, dill

Set the oven to 180°C/gas 4. Butter the insides of four large jam jars, add the seasoned cod fillets, dress with lemon juice and finish with a good knob of butter on each fish. Place a small piece of baking paper on top of each fish and bake the open jars for 10 minutes.

Remove the jars from the oven, quickly lay a blanket of the fine herbs on top of the fish, replacing the lids and leave them to rest for 10 minutes. Serve with new potatoes and dressed green salad, using maybe the jar juices as a dressing.

Cod baked under herbs

064

With the risk of being booed off the stage, this is my version of the infamous classic Danish dessert, *rødgrød med fløde*, knowing full well that I am tinkering with a tradition, with which I have no right to tinker. The last time I did anything so blasphemous was when I had just started as a chef at Søllerød Kro. After leaving Blighty it was my first position within a Danish kitchen. I was responsible for the fish, and on that particular day it was my turn to prepare the staff dinner. The day before I had asked what they would like for the evening's meal and nine out of ten asked for *boller i karry* (being meatballs in a curry sauce). Fine, I thought, I had ordered the goods and tackle, and started work. From home I brought my 'Green Street' Indian spice mixture (see page 153). I fried onions, garlic, green pepper and chilli. Browned the spices, added chicken stock and left the sauce to simmer for a couple of hours with freshly chopped tomato. Making small fine meatballs from veal and pork adding fresh ginger and coriander leaves, I carefully fried them and finished them off by simmering them gently within the thoroughly authentic sauce. Then I added okra, apple and peach, served with steamed rice pilaf spiced with turmeric, fresh coriander plus poppadoms, naan and mango chutney... all the staff except for one hated it! I had ruined a good Danish classic, complete and utterly, I was never forgiven.

And now I am doing the same with their holier-than-thou *rødgrød*, according to them a thick stew of red berries, thickened to billy-o with cornflour and served with milk... mmm! *A change seemed in order.*

I can't really give any quantities for this one, a gastronomic rule-of-thumb is needed here folks. The amount of berries depends on how many are going to eat it, the amount of sugar depends on the sweetness of the fruits used, the further on in the season the sweeter the fruit.

Rødgrød, my way is as follows – I refuse to cook the fruits, I just feel that the summer is lost when doing so. I just wash and pick strawberries, rinsing and removing stones from cherries, checking for grubs and any other creepy-crawlies that could be found within wild raspberries or blackberries. Pour all the prepared berries into a cooled bowl and crush them lightly with your fingers, sprinkle over a fine light cane sugar that has been crushed and flavoured with the seeds of a vanilla pod, taste, taste, taste... adding a touch more sugar if needed and a squeeze of lemon juice. Leave the berries to macerate for a couple of hours. Serve drowned within a pool of well chilled organic double cream.

Red heaven!

PS – if using rhubarb, you'll have to poach it tender first.

Red berries with cream HINDBÆR

065

Dream Para[

Closing my eyes, I dream that one day I'll be able to buy a small house in a small village, with friendly old people playing boules and drinking the local tipple. I dream that after a good lunch, with a little vino and a good cup of strong coffee, I'll fall asleep under the chestnut tree and be woken with a cup of tea (*an Englishman abroad*) by my beautiful wife.

Later we'll stroll through our olive grove and finish up at the village's only restaurant, which has incidentally been run by the same family for several happy generations. The place is simple and rustic, no airs-and-graces, no starred pretence. We'll have a small plate of baby vegetables from the restaurant's own garden – tiny carrots, fennel, tomatoes, sliced celery and green beans, drizzled with olive oil made from the olives of my own grove (apart from good karma, my only addition to the evening's proceedings). I don't produce too many bottles, a few for the restaurant, a few to send home to my pals in Copenhagen, Barcelona and Blighty, and the remaining bottles for us to pour over freshly made pasta or to enrich the recipe for my favourite Sicilian lemon-saffron cake. Having dipped our vegetables in a small bowl of the house's own aioli, we'll have a small buttered, grilled trout sprinkled with crisp toasted almonds, lemon and parsley. We can already smell the main course, spring lamb marinated with mountain thyme and wild rosemary, grilled over old vines. As usual at this time of the year we'll order the house *crema Catalana* with freshly picked strawberries and plumpest cherries – it does not get better than this, sweetened with local honey, creamy and rich with local farm cream, sharpened with the region's own oranges and lemons, we can see the trees, heavy with fruit, from where we sit. We share the dessert while we enjoy two small cups of coffee and I have a sip of my grappa, made also in the restaurant's own little cellar. Happy and full we'll walk home, it is not far. We water our flower pots and make sure that the dogs have a little in their bowls for the night. Close the shutters, kiss and close our tired eyes.

I don't quite know where it is, this Dream Paradise. Provence? Tuscany? Vilanova de Meià in Northern Spain?... for the moment it is but a dream.

I dream of Crema Catalana

066

FOR FOUR DREAMERS

CREAM
150 ml double cream
100 ml milk
200 g egg yolks
70 g honey
Juice and grated zest of 1 orange
Juice and grated zest of 1 lemon

GARNISH
1 large tray fresh strawberries, pitted cherries or raspberries –
    or all if poss!
Fresh tarragon leaves
Toasted almonds
A little olive oil
Black olives, stones removed and blanched in boiling water
    twice, then dried overnight in the oven at 50°C/gas ⅛, then
    finely chopped

Heat the cream and milk in a saucepan. Whisk egg yolks and honey until smooth. Pour the warmed cream-milk over the egg yolk-honey mixture whisking constantly as you go, cool a little. Add juice and zest from the orange and lemon, and leave the cream to infuse for three hours. Sieve and pour into an ovenproof dish. Place the dish in a bain marie and bake at 110°C/gas ¼ for about 30 minutes. Leave the cream to cool before serving, but it should not be put in the fridge!

Our crema Catalana Chez Paul is served caramelised with sugar in a small bowl with lovely strawberries, dressed with unfiltered olive oil, sprinkled with toasted, chopped almonds. Finished with tarragon leaves and dried, finely chopped black olives.

Gotland

On the website of Gotland's Tourist Office, it tells of this beautiful tiny Swedish island, once being adjoined to Australia – a 400 million year old yarn or the Gods-honest truth? Care I not, Gotland was indeed created by a blessed hand.

As far as I know, about almost everything which is grown and exported from the island is either organic or bio-dynamic, if not, it is indeed injected with the island's good karma and love. From Gotland we get everything from baby beetroots to mini celeriac, wild rocket and fantastic edible flowers, cheeses, honeys, mustards, oils and vinegars. At the top of our shopping list are their fantastic carrots – sweet, intense and crisp. Our 'lady' in Gotland is called Suzanne. Lovely Suzanne is devoted to her products. She packs her prized produce herself and it is flown down from Gotland to Henne Kirkeby Kro every Tuesday.

The following dish is a small fusion between our salt kitchen, and our sweet. During a long menu, served just after the meats, it's fresh and most invigorating, bridging the two kitchens, and preparing one for the desserts that follow.

Carrots from Gotland are rarely available on the shelves in Danish supermarkets. But carrots – and vegetables on the whole – from the amazing farmed area of Lammefjord for example, are also very good. I have even bought excellent organic carrots in Netto's discount store.

The carrots in the picture are, as far as the small ones are concerned, served raw and the larger ones are blanched in lightly salted water, still having their very crisp texture when served. The carrots have a dressing of the sea buckthorn berry – a tiny yellow-orange berry, extremely sharp, with very bitter tendencies, growing wild particularly in Sweden. Dried sea buckthorn and sea buckthorn juice are available from many Scandinavian health food shops, and online. Arrange, as in the picture, with granita, nougatine leaves and a few marjoram leaves.

MIDDLE COURSE FOR FOUR SUMMER WARM LOVELIES

4 brilliant carrots, different varieties and colours, if poss
   washed, peeled and cut
Fresh marjoram
A little rapeseed oil
Ice cold freshly squeezed orange juice seasoned with a little sea
   buckthorn juice and passed through a coffee filter

VINAIGRETTE
50 ml sea buckthorn juice
50 ml apple vinegar
200 ml cold pressed virgin rapeseed oil
100 ml olive oil
1 tbsp sugar
Sea salt

Whisk all the ingredients and season with a little sea salt.

ORANGE-SEA BUCKTHORN-GRANITÉ
100 g sugar
200 ml freshly squeezed orange juice
200 ml sea buckthorn juice

Dissolve the sugar in a little of the orange juice, and mix with the rest of the juice. Please do not warm all of the juice; the fresh orange acidity will be lost. Freeze the juice and then scrape it with a spoon to achieve the granita-like consistency. Have it ready in the freezer.

PINE NUT NOUGATINE
60 g sugar
3 tsp glucose
1 tbsp pine nuts, toasted and finely chopped

Boil sugar and glucose to a light caramel. Leave to cool and blend to a fine powder. Sieve evenly onto a flat oven tray lined with a silicone mat, sprinkle over the pine nuts. Place in the oven at 120°C/gas ½ until the powder has caramelised once again. Leave to cool and break into pieces.

The dish is served as a small fresh appetiser or palate cleanser after the main course. Dress the cut carrots with a little vinaigrette. Arrange in a small deep bowl with the granita, nougatine leaves and marjoram leaves. Finally pour over the juice – ice cold.

The 400 million year old carrots of Gotland

067

As a first course or as a cheese course – this sweet-sour-salty-crisp experience reminds me of Gotland's unspoilt nature. Are you the lucky owner of a Gotland truffle, then do not hold back with grating it, and everyday food will be lifted to the genuine gastronomy of the North.

FOR FOUR

200 ml apple vinegar
200 g honey
400 g beetroot – boiled tender in salted water
200 g sheep's milk cheese
2 slices of rye bread, roasted crisp in butter and made into
rather uneven crumbs

Boil the vinegar together with the honey. Peel the boiled beetroots and place into the warm marinade. You can, if necessary, cut them into smaller pieces if the beetroots are very large; leave to marinate at least overnight.

The following day serve the warmed beetroot with sheep's cheese at room temperature, dressed with rye bread buttered crumbs.

Sheep's milk cheese, beetroot & rye bread

068

The day we were hunting truffles in Gotland, Daisy, Suzanne's girlfriend's little white wonder of a dog, found no less than 14 truffles in 45 minutes. On the way home from the hunt she proudly posed for the camera in the back of the battered old delivery van. Proud she was of her new fans, glad we were to have met her. Her tight, small fine curls made her actually look more like a local Gotland lamb, was this a new kind of animal? I felt like Charles Darwin, I had lost my heart to Daisy.

FOR FOUR DAISY ADMIRERS

1 litre milk
4 fresh bay leaves
Sea salt
1 super celeriac – mine are from Suzanne, Queen of Gotland
2 tbsp good quality butter
1 Gotland truffle

Warm the milk with the bay leaves and season with sea salt. Peel the celeriac and cut into four. Gently cook the celeriac in the milk until tender, it should be slightly al dente.

Put the celeriac in soup plates. Remove the bay leaves and froth the milk to lighten. Check the seasoning and pour over the celeriac, dressing well with grated truffle.

Suzanne's celeriac in bay leaf milk with Daisy's truffles

069

Feddet
+ Gisselfeld

I have recently made a new friend. He is called Ivan, Ivan the Great of Feddet. He is a baron and owns a chunk of beautiful land in Southern Sjælland. Here he grows organic vegetables, herbs and flowers, and rides eco-friendly electric motor cross bikes in his spare time. His estate provides me with the most wonderful of produce. Wild herbs, fine shoots of spruce and sweetest raspberries, the blackest blackcurrants. But it was the blueberries that first caught my eye.

We used them every year, throughout their season at the restaurant. We made sorbets and ice cream, candied them and served them with roast duck and pigeon. We mashed them with a little local vinegar, poured over butter-roasted lobster. Marinated within their own juice with a little honey and wild thyme from Ivan's garden,

we served them with a small soft creamy goat's cheese, a little toasted rye bread and spoonful of rapeseed oil.

When you are on your way to Feddet from Copenhagen you will pass the spectacular gardens of Gisselfeld Cloister. Here live my beautiful pals Stig and Greg alongside their glorious glass construction, a true Victorian orangery, which houses a collection of wonderfully rare orchids, geraniums, flowers, exotic plants and trees, as well as olive, kumquat, lemon, lime, orange – a kickstart to my culinary fantasy every time I step inside their place.

Simply genuine, never overdone, but deep, fine and pure.... love you Flowerboys.

Blueberry sorbet & berries pickled with wild thyme

070

SORBET
300 g fresh blueberries
130 g sugar
120 ml water
30 g glucose
Zest of a ½ lemon

Wash the blueberries. Bring sugar and water to the boil, add glucose and let it dissolve. Whisk well and cool. Add blueberries and lemon juice, blend fine. Adjust the taste if needed.

Leave to cool completely before putting it in an ice-cream machine. If you do not have an ice-cream machine, pour the mixture into a bowl and place it in the freezer. Remove it from the freezer every 15 minutes and stir the mixture with a fork, continue stirring every 15 minutes until the sorbet has set.

BLUEBERRIES PICKLED WITH WILD THYME
200 ml water
200 g sugar
1 small bunch of thyme, wild if possible
200 g blueberries
Apple vinegar

Boil the water with the sugar and thyme. Leave the syrup to cool slightly before adding the blueberries, adding a dash of apple vinegar at the end giving a fresh sharp touch. Pour into scalded jam jars until needed.

Denmark's
west coast

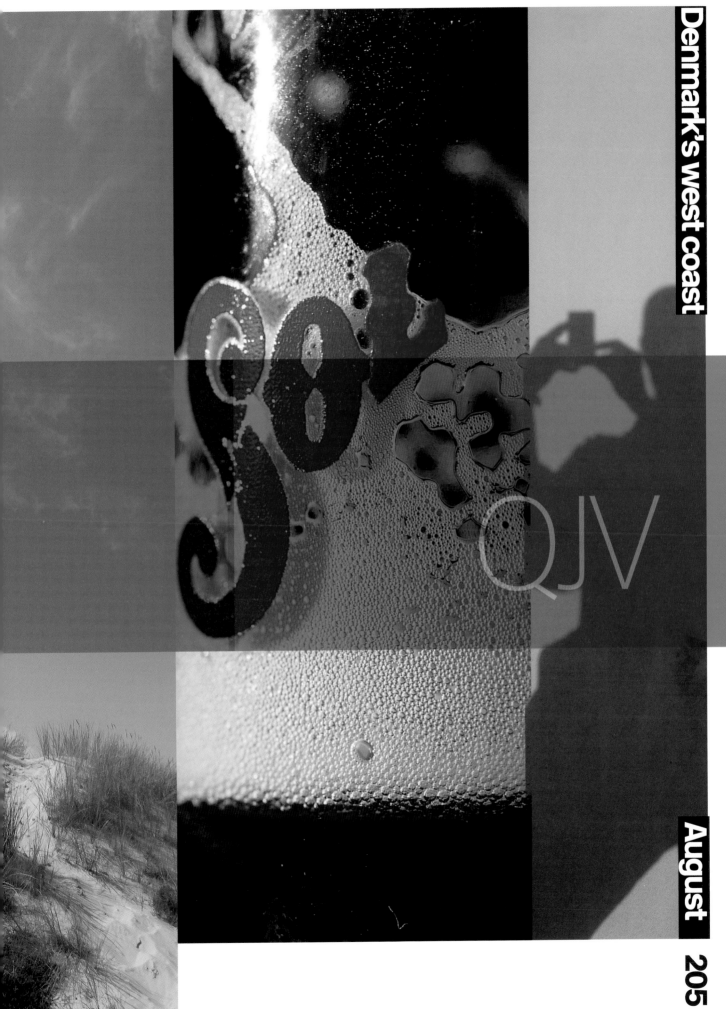

Chanterelles smoked in rosemary

071

Serve over toasted sourdough bread topped with a poached egg, or folded into fresh linguine, or chopped with ricotta as a filling for your ravioli. In an omelette with grated gruyère, or poised upon creamed potato. With butter-roasted turbot or large grilled rib-eye steak, or within a baguette with honey roast ham and mayo made with olive oil. Chopped to flavour soft butter, or to infuse a salad dressing. Sliced over an aged beef carpaccio with mature Parmesan, or with seared scallops and grilled lemon. Floating over a creamy chicken soup, or indeed with a roast chicken and a sharp cucumber salad, enhancing a chicken and asparagus vol au vent would also be nice. For primping a pizza with tomato and mozzarella, or on a slice of just-baked rye bread with a crumbling goat's cheese. Served warm in a chilled soup of fresh peas and mint, or served bound with a touch of sherry vinegar over grilled chorizo and a fried duck egg. Warmed in a little butter with asparagus with freshly cooked gnocchi, or mixed in a classic Caesar salad... *I could go on.*

Sauté a good handful of trimmed, washed and well dried chanterelles quickly in butter with a little garlic and a small stalk of rosemary, place into a scalded glass jar with a close fitting lid. Then warm a couple of rosemary sprigs in a dry pan until they start to smoke. Add to the chanterelles in the glass. Then close the lid tightly, trapping the rosemary-smoke inside. Leave the mushrooms to rest before using, at least two hours. Do not open the lid in the meantime.

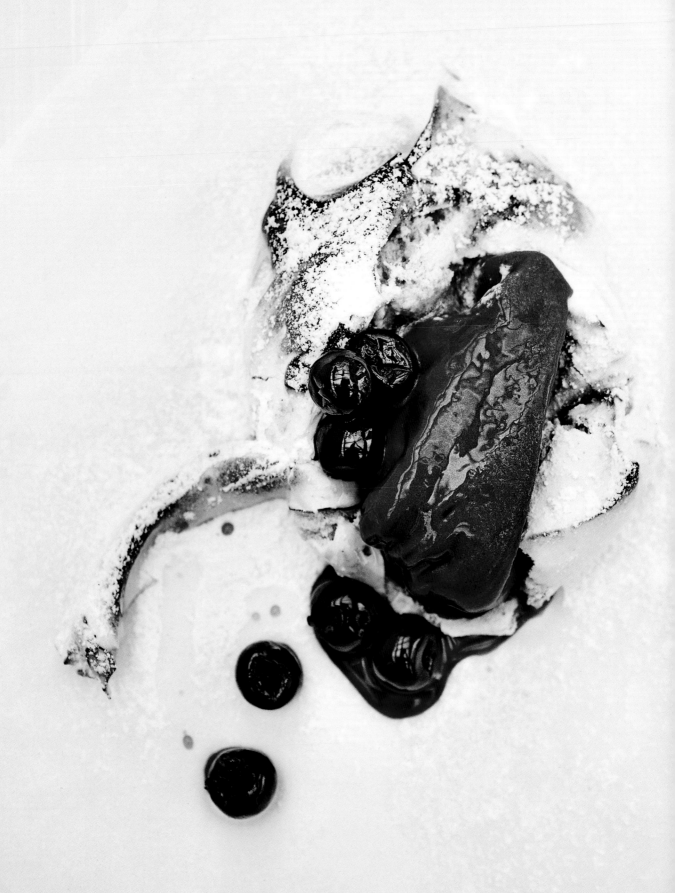

Crisp outside and chewy toffee-like inside, that is how meringues should be.

FOUR LARGE CHERRY MERINGUES

6 large egg whites
½ tsp fine sea salt
Seeds of 1 vanilla pod
200 g warm honey (approx. 120°C)
1 tsp cornflour
1 tsp white wine vinegar
2 tbsp cherry sorbet that has not yet gone through the ice-cream machine

CHERRY SORBET
300 g fresh cherries
150 g sugar
100 ml water
30 g glucose
Juice of a ½ lemon

Whisk the egg whites in a very clean, dry metal bowl until light and airy. Add the salt and vanilla seeds. Add the warm honey a little at a time while constantly whisking. Continue whisking until the mixture has cooled. Fold the cornflour, vinegar and 2 tbsp of cherry sorbet (see below) into the meringue mixture. Using a large spoon, or as I do, my hands, place large mountains of meringue onto a baking tray lined with baking paper or silicone, bake for 10 minutes at 140°C/gas 1 to start with, then for three hours at 50°C/gas ⅛.

I finish off by giving the meringue a little colour under the grill, this adds a caramel toffee-like, burnt note which I like very much.

Wash the cherries and remove the stones. Boil the sugar and water, add the glucose and leave to dissolve. Blend the cherries with this warm syrup and season with lemon juice. Pass the mixture through a sieve and leave to cool. Place and run in an ice-cream machine until firm.

Serve the sorbet over the just warm, crisp, chewy meringue.

Cherry meringues

072

Over on the west coast of Denmark's Jylland the beach is full of razor clams. They are called razor clams because they look like an old fashioned Sweeney Todd-style cut-throat razor. It is a pity that they are not more popular (the clam, that is), they're a top delicacy in Italy, Spain and Portugal. I hope that before long I will see more of these delicious creatures on the iced, marble slabs of our beloved fishmongers round the country.

The tiny, fine maritime herb in this dish is called poor man's asparagus in my home country. Salicornia Europaea, glasswort, samphire, sea fennel or salt herb. Samphire has an amazingly fresh and very intense taste of the sea. Tones of seaweed, green asparagus and maybe a little raw Savoy cabbage is also there somewhere. It reminds me of a summer's day on the beach, a morning dip with the wonderful zing, and feeling of sea water on the lips, dried by a warm summer breeze.

'Half-way down hangs one that gathers samphire, dreadful trade!'
William Shakespeare's *King Lear* (1592), act IV, scene 6

FROM A RAZOR-ADDICT, FOR FOUR

1 kg of super fresh razor clams (available from your local fishmonger but maybe you will need to give him a day or two to get hold of them)
4 cloves garlic
1 glass white wine
100 g butter
500 g samphire (ask your local fish-joe for this too)
A little sea salt
A little freshly squeezed lemon juice

Wash the clams thoroughly for sand. Place in a large saucepan or deep sauté pan with the finely sliced garlic and white wine. Put a lid on and steam them over a very high heat until they have all opened, for about five minutes. Discard any that have not opened. Throw in small cubes of cold butter together with the washed and trimmed samphire. Folding carefully together, season the sauce with sea salt and a little lemon juice. Serve immediately with some real good bread.

You could of course use blue mussels instead of razor clams, and maybe try the thin French wild asparagus, if you cannot get hold of samphire.

Razor clams with samphire

073

LÆSØSPRØTTEN

Served with newly dug potatoes rolled with butter and snipped lovage, a little lettuce drizzled with olive oil, mixed with crème fraîche, lemon juice and sea salt – your terraced summer evening will be blessed.

The first time I witnessed this dish was with Michel Michaud at his earlier restaurant, Marie Louise in the courtyard of Lotterups Gård, Odense. Michel is one of the biggest chefs we have here in Denmark, well maybe not in a physical sense, but a superchef with a capital S, that he is.

My time with Michel unfortunately didn't last very long. We knew each other really well before I started work there, and we are very, very close now. But to share a red hot kitchen with the great man for twelve hours every day, didn't really work out for any of us. Two Napoleons sharing the same 10 square metre battle-tent during the heat of service, pretty it was not..

Michel loves skate and so do I. It should be very fresh – ultra-fresh, if not, you'll know it by the aggressive kick of ammonia that wafts from its wings. The fish may be a little difficult to get hold of; a lot of our fishmongers will not sell it because ideally it should be caught, sold and eaten on the same day. In this recipe you can use practically any type of fish from our waters, for example sole, brill, gurnard or weaver fish, eel is also superb *grenobloise'd*!

Skate wings 'Grenobloise' Michel Michaud

074

FOR FOUR

4 skinned skate wings, each about 200 g
A little olive oil

GARNISH – BEURRE NOISETTE
200 g good quality butter
2 cloves garlic, sliced
2 shallots, finely chopped
4 tsp chopped capers
1 red chilli, seeds removed then finely chopped
1 small handful finely chopped flat leaf parsley
2 tomatoes, skinned and seeds removed, then cut into fine
**   cubes concassé**
Zest and segments of 2 lemons

Sea salt and freshly ground black pepper

Prepare the garnish and put to one side.

Brush the skate wings with a little olive oil and fry in a very hot non-stick frying pan, around two minutes on each side – not much longer. Keep the fish warm while you prepare the browned butter sauce, beurre noisette.

Heat the same pan, and throw in the butter letting it become brown and nutty, but do not let it burn. Pour the rest of the ingredients into the pan, toss them a little and pour the finished grenobloise garnish over the warm skate wings.

Yes, probably not the most typical of west coast Danish dishes but it tastes wonderful, and this is my book folks! If turbot is the King of fish, brill must *be* the Crown Prince. Rich, meaty and fantastically suited for roasting or grilling, try making fish and chips with brill or turbot, and you will never again make do with a member of the cod family. The dressing for this recipe is inspired by one of my friends, Christophe, who lives in sunny Provence. It has a happy positive feel to it, it tastes of sun. It'll warm your soul, on a not so sunny summer's day.

FOR FOUR

DRESSING
300 ml olive oil
100 ml red wine vinegar
2 cloves garlic
2 anchovy fillets in olive oil
½ chilli, seeds removed
½ grilled red pepper
2 sun-dried tomatoes, finely chopped
Zest of a ¼ orange
Zest of a ¼ lemon
1 star anise
10 coriander seeds, crushed
10 fennel seeds, crushed
1 sprig oregano
1 sprig marjoram
1 sprig rosemary
1 sprig thyme
1 tsp sugar
Sea salt

4 thick fillets of fresh brill or turbot – you could also use any
other white fish, scallops, langoustines and lobster
Olive oil
1 clove garlic
1 sprig thyme
Sea salt
1 small bunch small summer onions
2 artichokes, trimmed and cut into quarters
12 semi-dried tomatoes

Gently warm all of the dressing ingredients together and leave to just tick over for 30 minutes. Jar, and refrigerate to infuse overnight if possible.

Roast the seasoned fish, til golden in a little olive oil with garlic and thyme. Warm the dressing and pass it through a sieve. Grill the trimmed summer onions and artichokes, slice the semi-dried tomatoes and add to the warm dressing. Serve over the warm fish – fresh herbs or crisp fried sage leaves would also be very nice.

BRANDADE
In the picture I've garnished the dish with a little brandade. Eight lightly crushed new potatoes are bound with four tablespoons (100 g) of well rinsed, bay leaf-milk-poached salt cod. Gently fork together and season with black pepper, lemon juice and lots of olive oil.

Brill 'Provençale'

075

This recipe works just as well with sole, plaice, cod or brill, haddock, skate, langoustine, lobster or monkfish. And the same applies to the herbs. I've used wild wood sorrel here that gives a wonderful sharp, lemony edge, but parsley, tarragon, chervil or dill would also be superb.

FOR FOUR PEOPLE

100 g butter
1 large sole, cut into fillets
Sea salt
100 g fresh chanterelles, plus a little butter for roasting
1 shallot, finely chopped
1 clove garlic, crushed
1 tbsp small capers
Lemon juice
1 handful fresh herbs of your choice – wild if possible

Turn the oven to 180°C/gas 4. Melt the butter in a pan until golden brown and having a nut-caramel-like aroma. Remove the pan from the heat and pass the butter through a fine sieve, discarding the milk solids.

Brush the sole fillets with the browned butter and sprinkle with sea salt. Bake for four to five minutes. Remove from the oven and keep warm under foil.

In a hot pan roast the chanterelles with a knob of butter, finely chopped shallot, garlic and capers. Finally season with a little squeeze of lemon juice and a little sea salt. Pour over the fish and dress with fine herbs.

Dover sole in browned butter with chanterelles

076

Læsø

A while ago now on a Saturday evening, after over sixty hungry guests and a busy night with our beloved Chef's Table – unexpected vegetarians, vegans and other unusual unexplained requests that make us cooks extra happy, whist dancing around in the heat of our kitchen – we finally turned off our dear Molteni, polished the last of the coppers and eventually received our little glass of wine (and maybe a beer or two) as the town square bell rang 2am.

Five hours later I stood in the somewhat Lilliput'esque airport of Roskilde with my son of seven years. We were on our way to the island of Læsø in Alex's tiny, Lego-like twin-prop aeroplane. Alex looks like a real pilot with the biggest, most well kept, glazed handlebar moustache that I have seen to this day. After a short hour, through the silver grey rainclouds we soon saw the beautiful green woodland of Læsø, perched to the north-eastern coast of Jylland. Læsø Langoustine Festival is held at Østerby harbour every year at the beginning of August – and for the first time in 2004. Amongst other events they invite professional chefs over to battle for the prize of The Golden Langoustine Claw. We were four that year, given the task of creating a course using the island's products. We scoured the beaches, forests and local farms – langoustine should of course, play the leading roll. Most happy indeed was I in 2004 to bring home the 'Claw' after I presented a dish using the gargantuan langoustines, warmed with locally salted speck and raspberries from the mayor's very own back garden. The dish was strewn with wild flower petals and hedgerow herbs. A little soup of the beast's head was flavoured with tiny buttered chanterelles, served in the handmade coffee cups of the island's salt-marsh-master, Poul.

August 2006... 12 o'clock on a Sunday. We stood again on the harbour, in front of 300 wild langoustine lovers. Freshened by the light summer rain – locally shot rabbit and fresh langoustines were placed over warm coals and local vines. My plates were dressed with the fennel aioli and my green tomato and apple compote, I was raring to go – I glanced around to check on my sous-chef of the day (Christian my son) – only to see tears running down his blushing cheeks. Not only had he cut the fennel finer that fine, his little finger had somehow come between his knife and the chopping board. The public gasped as we ran from the harbour in search of the nearest first-aid lady... exactly 3 minutes later we were ready again to climb the steps and return to the stage – tears dried and finger well plastered... it was like David Beckham returning to the field after an injury – the crowd went wild! Christian looked out from the stage to his people... looked down at his finger, and slowly raised his right hand – saluting and thanking HIS public.

Our grilled rabbit and langoustine with fennel and green tomato chutney was devoured by the jury. A few hours afterwards Christian and I were called up to receive again, the infamous Golden Langoustine Claw for 2006.

'The sympathy vote of the public had no influence what-so-ever!'

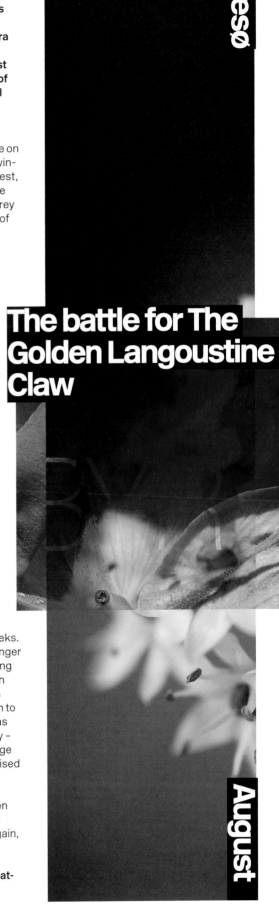

The battle for The Golden Langoustine Claw

FOR FOUR

4 large and super fresh Læsø langoustines
2 saddles of rabbit, boned
Læsø sea salt
1 tsp fennel seeds, toasted in a dry pan and crushed
Cold pressed rapeseed oil

CHUTNEY
4 green tomatoes, cut into cubes
2 green apples, cut into cubes
2 shallots, finely sliced
100 g sugar
100 ml apple vinegar
1 tsp fennel seeds, toasted in a dry pan and crushed

AIOLI
4 new potatoes, cut into cubes
1 fennel, sliced
2 cloves garlic, crushed
100 ml mayonnaise (preferably homemade, made from olive oil)
1 tbsp pastis
Lemon juice
Sea salt

SALAD
1 fennel bulb
1 handful rocket
Cold pressed rapeseed oil
Lemon juice
Sea salt

Start by making the chutney. Boil the tomatoes and apples together with shallot, sugar, apple vinegar and fennel seeds. Give it 10 minutes at full heat, stirring continuously for the chutney to reduce, thick and shiny.

Then boil the potatoes for the aioli with the sliced fennel, when tender blend thoroughly. Mix with garlic and mayonnaise. Season to taste with a little pastis, lemon juice and sea salt.

Season the langoustines and rabbit with a little sea salt and fennel seeds. Dress with a little rapeseed oil and leave the flavours to infuse for a while. Grill the rabbits to medium rare and the langoustines to rare over hot coals.

Serve the grilled rabbit and langoustine with chutney, aioli and a crudité of fennel and rocket dressed with rapeseed oil, lemon juice and sea salt. Dress the finished plates with a little extra sea salt and fennel seeds, a little lemon juice and rapeseed oil.

Grilled rabbit & Læsø langoustine

077

Bornholm

Delicious Bornholm

It is always the simple things in life that attract me to the Baltic island of Bornholm. A slice of rye bread with smoked herring and a cold lager. Fish cakes *frikadeller* with fresh herbs and homemade remoulade. Freshly caught, sparkling plaice, so fresh that it curls on the hot pan... capers, parsley and lemon.

That is Bornholm, and that is precisely what makes this crazy culinary world worth spending energy on.

Bornholm is of course not Barcelona, when it comes to the number of decent places to eat, but they are there. Kadeau near Aakirkeby, is such a place. The little white wooden summerhouse, so pretty, idyllic in every way, and the location is in a league of its own with an uninterrupted view of the Baltic Sea. The experience with my pal Rasmus at the helm is worth the long sail to the island in itself, and the food is sharp, fresh, deep and full of flavour.

Gratin of smoked mackerel, new potatoes & chives

078

FOR FOUR

250 ml beautiful double cream
Sea salt and freshly ground black pepper
Lemon juice
6 egg yolks
2 handfuls new potatoes, poached tender in salted water
1 large smoked mackerel, filleted and bones removed
Radishes, onions, chives and flowers

Gently warm the cream, remove from the heat and season with salt, pepper and lemon juice. Whisk in two of the egg yolks. Crush the potatoes lightly between your finger and thumb, arrange them with the mackerel. Add an egg yolk to the middle of each plate. Divide the seasoned cream among the plates and bake in a hot oven or under a warm grill until golden brown.

Dress with clipped chives and serve with lots of bread, and a well chilled Bornholm ale.

Autumn

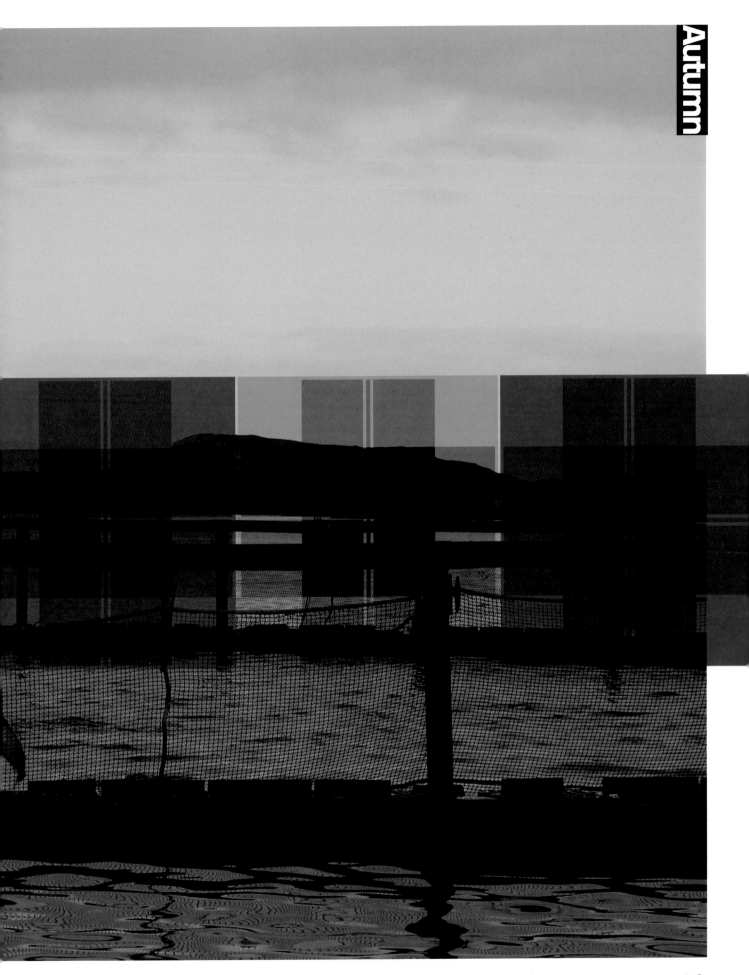

Scotland

September came and Scotland called. Via Glasgow we flew towards the Outer Hebrides, which lie like a shelter towards the rebellious Atlantic, north-west of the mainland.

Whilst in Glasgow we had a late Indian meal of lamb biriyani and tandoori chicken with spiced naan, daal and raita. Quenching our thirst with iced Kingfisher beer, before tea with coconut kulfi arrived. My travel companions were rather downhearted, having arrived in Scotland without having eaten either haggis, or the infamous deep fried Mars bar.

Early the next morning we boarded the little propeller plane to the island of Benbecula, just to the south of Harris (of tweed jacket fame). We were flying low over what must have been thousands of tiny islands. I imagined all the whisky houses below us, it was almost as if the smoky aromas of peat and oak were seeping into the plane, and our already high expectations were in no way watered.

We landed on, what seemed like, a deserted island and were met by Angus the organic salmon king of the area. We were packed into his well-aged van and rushed away over the island to visit the nets. The heather-clad landscape was wonderful, wild and rough. It wasn't too difficult to imagine the great William Wallace with his blue-painted face galloping after the latest English intruder ...FREEEEDOM!

From Angus' rubber speed boat we saw the salmon from afar, jumping from the ponds, full of life, a magnificent sight. Later we rushed back to the mainland, most hungry indeed. There is nothing like a good soup to satisfy your appetite, your body and your soul, and, well, as far as I'm concerned it does not matter what type of soup it is, as long as it's piping hot and homemade (Heinz tomato soup being an exception to the rule). In no time, I'd downed my vegetable-laden Scottish broth and the warm highland cheese buttered scones were amazing alongside a small dram, or two of jolly highland spirit.

Scotland the Brave

BEB

My previous dram together with the broth wasn't the only fair cup during our trip; in fact I don't really remember too much of our time in bonny Scotland, you could say that the superb Scottish single-malt whisky made an indelible impression on us fair gentlemen. My porridge the next morning was laden with the stuff, brown sugared and creamy, it was truly luuverly... For lunch, Angus' salmon was brushed with the island glory before being carefully smoked over a gentle fire of local heather, and glass after glass came to the table in the evening while we chatted in the hotel bar with *Angus the Brave* before retiring to our pits.

It was a quick stop in Glasgow on the way home – haggis was found, hunted, slaughtered, enjoyed... being naturally washed down with one last little cup of golden whisky.

Scotland, land of my forefathers, was indeed most grand.

HOT SMOKED SALMON FOR FOUR

500 g organic salmon fillet, wild salmon or Baltic salmon if possible
Sea salt
100 ml Scottish whisky
Wood chippings from pine or oak, for example
1 large handful freshly cut wild heather
1 small smoking oven (available from your local fishing/hunting shop) or a kettle grill

Begin with salting the salmon well and leaving it to infuse with the whisky for one, maybe two hours.

If you are using a kettle grill light it with a few charcoals. When it is ready, place a foil tray of wood chippings in the embers. When it starts to smoke, move the tray a little away from the hottest embers and place the heather in the tray. Place the fish on the grate and close the lid on the grill, leaving the fish to hot smoke for 15-20 minutes.

If you are using a smoking oven, you only need to light it with wood chippings and heather at the bottom and follow the instructions.

Serve with buttered boiled potatoes and a green salad with *mormor* dressing made from cream flavoured with a good splash of lemon juice and sea salt, a Danish grandmother classic.

Angus' heather smoked salmon

079

A cold autumn evening on the sofa in front of a roaring fire. Inspector Jack Frost on the TV, the children gone to bed and the red wine open. *Bon appétit.*

FOR FOUR OR SIX JACK FROST-FANS

500 g venison, neck or shoulder cut into large cubes
100 g smoked bacon, cut into small cubes
Butter
4 shallots, finely sliced
1 tsp finely chopped rosemary
1 tsp fresh thyme leaves
Zest of a ½ orange
50 ml Scotch whisky
2 glasses red wine
1 litre game stock
80 g finely chopped dark chocolate
Salt and pepper
1 tray of blackberries

Brown the meat very well with the bacon in a little butter and oil. Add the shallots, rosemary, thyme and orange zest, again colouring well. Flambé the pot with the whisky, pour the wine in and gently reduce. Pour the stock over and leave to simmer for two hours over gentle heat.

When the meat is tender, remove it from the pot. Turn up the heat and reduce the sauce until strong and sticky. At this point the sauce must not be re-boiled, whisk with the chocolate and season to taste with salt and pepper. Fold in the blackberries, returning also the meat to the saucepan.

Serve with mashed potatoes, creamy polenta, baked root vegetables or steamed pearl barley with lashings of butter.

Venison, blackberries & chocolate

080

It doesn't get more Scottish than this. It is the essence of Scotland, the very thing that Braveheart was made of. (If we ignore the fact that the role was played by Mel Gibson who, as we know, is an *Aussie!*)

FOR FOUR OR SIX BRAVE HEARTS

1 large pheasant
100 g smoked bacon, cut into cubes
Butter
4 shallots, finely chopped
1 carrot, cut into fine cubes
¼ celeriac, cut into fine cubes
1 parsnip, cut into fine cubes
2 large sprigs of thyme
2 large sprigs of rosemary
4 fresh bay leaves
100 g pearl barley
500 ml concentrated chicken stock
500 ml game stock
Salt and pepper
Freshly chopped lovage and parsley

Remove the legs from the pheasant and brown them with the bacon in a little butter. Add the shallots, herbs and the vegetables, sauté a little. Add pearl barley together with the two stocks. Leave to simmer under a lid for 30 minutes. Remove the thighs, leave to cool a little, and then pick the meat off the bone. Return the thigh meat to the soup and season to taste with salt and pepper.

Season the pheasant breast and fry it on the carcass in butter. Doing it this way you have more control over the roasting, which is most important, since it can quickly become dry.

Leave the breast to rest a little before cutting if off the carcass. Arrange the broth in deep plates with the sliced pheasant breast. Dress the broth well with lovage and parsley, drizzling with a little of the cooking juices.

Scotch broth

081

Maybe I should have written this recipe on the 31st October. A dark little devil like this would have been a most fitting finale to a dark and spooky Halloween feast – beginning with a wonderful first course of a creamed pumpkin soup whisked with fresh Parmesan and sprinkled with crisp salty pumpkin seeds. Then you will need to put your warm clothes on and go out in the garden to finish the main course of spit-roast suckling pig, adorned in a sticky marinade of honey, rosemary and black pepper with buttered Savoy cabbage and mashed potato. And finally, a dessert – blackened, liquorice parfait with blackberries and olives. Is this Halloween or what?

FOR SIX PEOPLE

BERRIES AND OLIVES
50 g black olives, stones removed
100 g honey
50 g brown sugar
Seeds of 1 vanilla pod
2 liquorice roots
Zest of ½ lemon
Approx. 400 g of dark berries, for example blackberries, blackcurrants, and blueberries
Black sesame seeds
100 ml olive oil

Bring the stoned olives quickly to the boil, drain, and dry well – this removes a fair deal of the salt. Dry them overnight in an oven set at 50°C/gas ⅛. Jar them, airtight until needed.

Warm the honey in a saucepan with the brown sugar, vanilla seeds and the liquorice roots, adding also the lemon zest. Cool slightly and macerate the berries in the mixture together with the olive oil.

LIQUORICE PARFAIT
700 ml double cream
8 large egg yolks
75 g sugar
1 tsp of liquorice powder (available from specialist grocers or sometimes at the pharmacy)
Seeds of 1 vanilla pod

Whisk the cream so that it is airy, and forms soft peaks. Whisk the egg yolks, sugar, liquorice powder, and vanilla seeds to an airy, creamy mix. Carefully fold in the whipped cream. Pour the liquorice cream into a suitable plastic container, place into the freezer for 4-5 hours until firm.

Remove the parfait from the freezer 10 minutes before serving. Slice and arrange the parfait, covered with the macerated dark berries, dressed with a little of the dried crushed olives and black sesame seeds.

Dress with a little olive oil and serve *ghoulishly*.

Liquorice parfait with blackberries & olives

082

New York

The strangest hotel, rustic and most spartan, basic to say the least with (in my opinion) the rudest of receptionists – or was it art?

The Gershwin Hotel situated at 27th Street and 5th Avenue, five minutes from everything. Five minutes from Soho, Chinatown and the villages of East, West and Greenwich. Five minutes stroll from Times Square and Central Park would be no longer on a pushbike.

The hotel with all of its old-world charm, seems to be the real-deal when looking for that genuine old New York apartment style. As I said, spartan. The Gershwin opened a little more than a hundred years ago and is somewhat of a little Mecca for the creative, arty-farty, photo-arts and music people, bearing their iPhones, iPads and macbooks. Money we have not, but of course, when in NYC one must sleep on Manhattan. My missus wasn't too keen, but all in all, I felt that it was a fine quirky little hotel, particularly when you consider that it costs less than a hundred quid per room-per night. Maybe that is why the receptionist's feel free attitude came over so less than friendly... unfriendly maybe it wasn't, was I maybe a witness to a piece of performance art?

Service at Spring Street's Balthazar was, on the other hand, a completely different story. During the five days I was in New York that time, I frequented the high hall of Balthazar four times, and all four times were experiences in themselves. Perfect brasserie-like food, hand-in-hand with a super cool, tip-top professional George Clooney – charming service. The kitchen is open from seven'ish in the morning until two at night, seven days a week. There are six menus, one for breakfast, one for brunch and another for lunch. Afternoon menu, dinner menu and a special one for afterhours-nightowls. I can tell you now my lovelies, I have eaten in many, many fantastic restaurants and read my way through many, many fantastic menus, but at Balthazar I wanted to eat all the dishes on all the menus, I could indeed live there. Breakfast is so fantastic that I had to hide and try the brunch. The lunch dishes are to die for, which quickly led to afternoon tea-time. Dinner, fabulous... night-time at Balthazar is absolutely at the top of my list next time I'm in New York.

I was inspired by all the wonderful food I had in New York City. New Yorkers love ham and when they discover that you come from the homeland of the ham they go berserk. I've tasted sweet mustard smothered salted ham at the loudest of New York delis, had braised, super spiced pulled ham in a Cuban sandwich at a rather nice gastro pub in Greenwich Village, and I tried USA's answer to Extremadura's blackfooted Iberico ham in one of the world's best restaurants, Per Se at Central Park... this being only rivalled by Dan Barber's ham, sliced like tissue over toast at his infamously secret Blue Hill restaurant at Stone Barns, a short train ride from Central Station. People, I tell you, I witnessed magic the night I ate the ham at Balthazar served as Eggs Benedict. It was salted, boiled and smoked over apple wood. Afterwards it had been sliced thinly and draped over crisp toasted English muffins, two perfect beautiful, sunny-smiling poached eggs were placed on top, covered with a warm velvety carpet of sauce hollandaise. *Oh Yeah!*

'HAM, HAM, GOOD FOR YOU MAN'

1 beautiful pork thigh from a decidedly happy pig, about 700 g
50 cloves
4 heaped tbsp Dijon mustard
4 heaped tbsp brown sugar
1 tsp freshly ground black pepper
500 ml water
Juice and finely grated zest of 2 large oranges, keep separate
Sea salt for boiling

Simmer the thigh in well salted water until tender, for about 1½ hours. Leave to cool in the water. Score the fat of the ham with small crosses and place a clove between each cross.
Warm together the mustard, the sugar, pepper, water and orange juice. Turn the heat down a little and leave the ham to simmer in the syrup for at least 1½ hours – basting and turning as often as you can, it will only get better. The syrup should be reduced by now, intense, sticky and honey- like, if not, remove the ham and reduce the sauce to the correct consistency. Sprinkle the ham with grated zest of the oranges and leave to infuse, in the syrup, overnight, in the fridge.

Enjoy the ham cold, thinly sliced, and served in a delicious sandwich with a little mayonnaise, tomatoes, salad and crisp cornichons. Or do as they do at Balthazar, *à la Benedict.*

Sugar-glazed ham à la beautiful Balthazar

083

Would you spend 25,000 dollars on a dessert? If yes is your answer then you should have gotten your butt down to New York's own Serendipity 3. A few years ago they were known for having the world's most expensive dessert on their menu, consisting of premium cocoa beans for making chocolate, flown in from fourteen different nations. The chocolate being baked into cakes, churned into ice creams and sorbets, whipped into mousse and creams and then endowed with five grams of 24 carat gold per portion. The desserts were topped with whipped cream and dressed with grated fresh truffle and gold leaf, served in a cut-crystal goblet, and decorated with more gold and 1 carat diamonds... naturally eaten with a gold spoon. Luckily enough for my bank balance I never was able to secure a reservation.

Only in America, folks!

Our golden chocolate bar at The Paul was not quite as extravagant as the creation of Serendipity, but it's not bad. A crisp, herbed butter shortbread base is spread with a lightly salted old fashioned English caramel toffee seasoned well with fresh winter truffles from the village of Alba, in Northern Italy. Piped with a topping of dark, intense Scharffen Berger chocolate mousse. Sliced into bars and lowered into a lacquer-like chocolate gelée, dusted with nine carat gold and sprinkled with a little French sea salt.

We use a square steel frame measuring exactly 25 x 25 cm and 5 cm high. When the bars have been cut and trimmed the recipe makes 22 pieces, each approx. 50 g... very precise I know, but this folks, is no cheap recipe. An investment it is, but, worth it, you are.

SHORTBREAD BASE
225 g plain flour
160 g unsalted butter
80 g egg yolk – *yes, I know it's weird to weigh egg but here it's important*

Mix the pastry quickly in a food processor. Film and refrigerate for at least two hours. Roll out the shortbread to the frame's dimensions, chill again for 15 minutes. Prick well with a fork and bake at 150°C/gas 2 for 25-30 minutes.

SALTED TRUFFLE TOFFEE
240 g brown sugar
250 g salted butter
4 tbsp honey
2 tbsp finely chopped fresh winter truffle

Warm the brown sugar, butter and honey to 125°C, for 5 minutes. Leave the mixture to cool a little and then fold in the finely chopped truffles. Pour the warm toffee into the frame, evenly over the baked shortbread base.

MOUSSE
200 g egg whites – *again my lovelies, weighing the whites will give you a better result, the size of egg whites and yolks differ tremendously*
80 g sugar
300 g dark chocolate 70% – if you can, Scharffen Berger chocolate is great
100 ml egg yolks
100 ml whipping cream

Whisk whites and sugar until stiff to form a meringue. Melt the chocolate and quickly whisk in the yolks. Fold the mixture into the meringue. Whisk the cream to soft-peak and fold into the chocolate/meringue mixture. Pour the mousse over the toffee, into the frame. Film and place into the freezer overnight.

CHOCOLATE GELÉE
450 ml water
370 g sugar
80 g glucose
150 g great cocoa powder
250 ml whipping cream
60 g dark chocolate 70%, melted over a bain marie
16 gelatine leaves, dissolved in water
1 pinch of edible gold dust

Carefully, carefully bring the water, sugar, glucose, cocoa and cream to the boil, for 15 minutes, whisking until thick. Take care, it burns easily! Remove from the heat. Fold in the melted chocolate, the leaf gelatine and the gold dust and whisk thoroughly. Keep the gelée warm, at around 25°C, but please try to be as precise as possible.

TO FINISH
A few sea salt crystals
A little gold leaf

Remove the frame from the freezer and rest for about ten minutes at room temperature. Cut into 20'ish equal sized bars, each 2 cm x 10 cm. Make sure the edges are nicely trimmed. Dip each bar quickly into warm chocolate gelée and put in the freezer again. Serve the chocolate with the chill taken off, sprinkled with a pinch of sea salt and a little extra gold leaf.

Our little gold bar

084

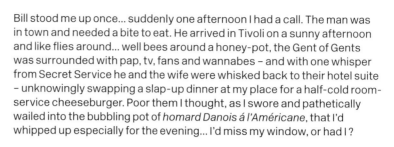

Bill stood me up once... suddenly one afternoon I had a call. The man was in town and needed a bite to eat. He arrived in Tivoli on a sunny afternoon and like flies around... well bees around a honey-pot, the Gent of Gents was surrounded with pap, tv, fans and wannabes – and with one whisper from Secret Service he and the wife were whisked back to their hotel suite – unknowingly swapping a slap-up dinner at my place for a half-cold room-service cheeseburger. Poor them I thought, as I swore and pathetically wailed into the bubbling pot of *homard Danois á l'Américane*, that I'd whipped up especially for the evening... I'd miss my window, or had I?

A few short seasons later the jungle drums boomed and the grapevines chattered that once more President Clinton could be visiting our fair city. The call came, and his visit was confirmed. A somewhat euphoric atmosphere spread once again through the house, although this time things were certainly kept hush, hush, everything was a little less formal. I spotted fewer armed suits, with snails in their ears, this time. Those that did turn up seemed to spend more time chatting up my line of lovely waitresses, than looking after *The Guvnor*.

Fifty-odd VIP's were invited to a cocktail reception at the restaurant, everyone having the opportunity to be photographed with the man. I said to my client that I'd do the job only if I'd get the same chance. Agreed this was and I was placed at the back of the queue, the only instruction being that I wasn't to converse with him, he just doesn't have the time. As I got closer, my confidence rose. It's my house, I thought, and this doesn't happen every day. What was the worst that could happen... *well they could shoot me I suppose.*

'Hello and welcome to my happy home, Mr. President', I proclaimed, whilst thrusting a copy of my latest cookbook into his free hand.
'Your home? What do you mean – your home?' he replied.
'Do you think, sir, that I wear this blue and white dress for fun?' I blabbered.
'You're *THE* Paul?' he asked excitedly.
'Yes Sir... err Mr. President, I'm The Paul', I replied, proud as the proudest peacock.

It was in every way a superb day. Made even better when a couple of weeks later I was sitting with my people one afternoon, having a bite to eat, fish *frikadeller* with tartare sauce and white cabbage salad. Flicking through the day's post, and among many dull letters there was one from New York, in a fine little cream-coloured envelope. Noticing not, the massive golden eagle on the back, I opened the envelope – it was from none other than the President himself. He thanked me for the warm welcome he had received with us and was looking forward to visiting us again one day. He also thanked me for the book which he thought was beautiful, but which required translation before he could start on the recipes. A proud Paul finished his fish dish with a small tear in the corner of his eye. One of the world's busiest men had sat down and written a personal thank you letter to little-old-me.

When this little book arrives back from the printers, I will sent that splendid gent my second copy – the first one I am afraid is reserved for *me dear old mum*.

When The Paul met
The Bill

Lobster à l'Américaine

FOR ME, THE PRESIDENT AND TWO BUDS

2 superb lobsters – alive and kicking!
4 tbsp olive oil
1 clove garlic
2 shallots, finely chopped
4 tbsp brandy
4 tomatoes, cut into small cubes
1 tbsp tomato puree
100 ml double cream
100 g cold butter, cut into small cubes
Sea salt and freshly ground black pepper
Lemon juice and a touch of Tabasco

Kill the lobsters swiftly, halve and crack the claws with the back of a heavy kitchen knife. Brown the lobsters well in a little olive oil with the crushed garlic and chopped shallots. Flambé the lobster with brandy, when the flames die, remove the lobster from the saucepan and keep warm.
Add the tomatoes, puree and whipping cream to the pan, bring to the boil, reduce the heat and simmer for 10 minutes, reducing gently and intensifying the flavours. Whisk the sauce with the cold butter, giving a velvet-like feel and shine. Season the sauce carefully with sea salt, fresh pepper, a squeeze of lemon and a touch of Tabasco.

Warm the lobster through the sauce and serve immediately with a big fat Napa Valley Chardonnay, a mighty Meursault or better still a rich *Cali chard*.

... written with great respect Sir, see you soon.

Elvis' last sandwich

086

You would have thought that Elvis, with all that cash, and all of those supposed friends and advisors, would have maybe eaten just a little bit better... unfortunately for the world, he didn't. Maybe it was just typical of the time, the 70's isn't exactly known as a gastronomic era, not too exciting to say the least.

As far as the recipe goes, I won't recommend that you eat this sweet little rocker too often. It is bombastic, it is evil, well, in fact it is so f++king bad, it's good.

HUNKS OF CARAMELISED LOVE, FOR FOUR DIE-HARD ELVIS FANS

4 eggs
Seeds from 1 vanilla pod
4 tbsp light brown sugar
100 ml whipping cream
Zest of 1 lemon
4 thick slices of fresh brioche or crust-free sourdough
Butter for frying
Smooth peanut butter
4 generous scoops of a really good vanilla ice cream
1 tray of fresh raspberries, macerated with 2 tbsp light brown sugar

Whisk the eggs, vanilla, sugar, whipping cream and lemon zest well. Dip the brioche slices in the mixture, and let them soak for a little while, turning now and then. Drain them a little and fry the slices in hot butter, on both sides until golden brown. Butter with a generous amount of peanut butter and serve with a large scoop of vanilla ice cream. Mash the raspberries lightly with a fork and spoon over.

SORRY FOLKS... Elvis has left the building

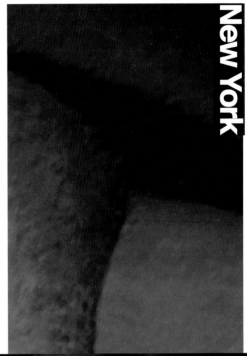

My, not-unlike-Hemingway-looking, pal Mikkel and I love the simple things in life... the world's best chocolate being one of them. With their hippie connections in California, the lovely Scharffen Berger folk make wonderful chocolate especially for people who just love good chocolate. A simple little fusion of love and chocolate that makes us most happy indeed.

500 g Scharffen Berger dark chocolate, of at least 70% cocao
350 g honey
Brilliant Scharffen Berger cocoa powder

Melt the chocolate and honey together, gently in a bain-marie. Pour the mixture into a tray or mould, leave to cool, cover and refrigerate overnight.

Warm a knife blade under the hot tap and dry with a tea towel between each cut, cutting the chocolate toffee into small slate-like slices. Roll the pieces in cocoa powder and enjoy them with a good cup of coffee.

Mikkel's Scharffen Berger chocolate-honey-toffee

087

Alba

Bianco d

We arrived early in the morning in the still-misty town of Alba and went straight to the nearest café to have breakfast, not caring if our eggs were fried, scrambled, boiled, poached or deep-fried, all that mattered was the fact that they would be covered in the new season's harvest of fresh truffle... they indeed were.

Anders, Christian and I, like excited schoolboys, waited with baited breath at the thought of the day's first truffle treat. Piping hot lightly fried eggs, swimming in browned butter under a duvet of grated black truffle... just thinking of it brings tears to my eyes. It was like Christmas morning, like seeing West Ham win the F.A. Cup *again*, like all my birthdays in one.

But from then on our morning went seriously downhill. It was Tuesday and without telling us, the truffle market in Alba had decided to close, holy-truffle-Tuesday it was, devastated we were. Downhearted and depressed, in desperation I grabbed my phone and called Sergio, my truffle-pusher in Copenhagen, maybe he could save the day.

Eledio, Sergio's truffle bloke in Alba, a man in his 70's, lives up in the mountains, and didn't speak a word of English. We called him and got hold of his son-in-law, shortly afterwards. GPS set, we were on our way to Eledio's secret hideout. After some time we found the winding road which led up the mountain, just outside the village of Monticello d'Alba, further on our eyes caught the sight of a man, waving frantically at our car. The son-in-law introduced us to the man. Eledio was indeed a truffle-king, as we had imagined, weather beaten, and wise, in touch with nature and his inner truffle, bloody hell he looked like a truffle!

We had no expectations of our visit, other than perhaps we might be allowed to see a few prized truffles... Instead we had an experience which we will never ever forget.

Eledio had, at very short notice, put his whole family to work. We were directed into the dining room with a view of the valley and then lunch was served. Marinated salads and vegetables from his own garden, Mama's fresh pasta with butter and grated white truffle. Fruit steeped within his own homemade sweet liqueur and coffee.

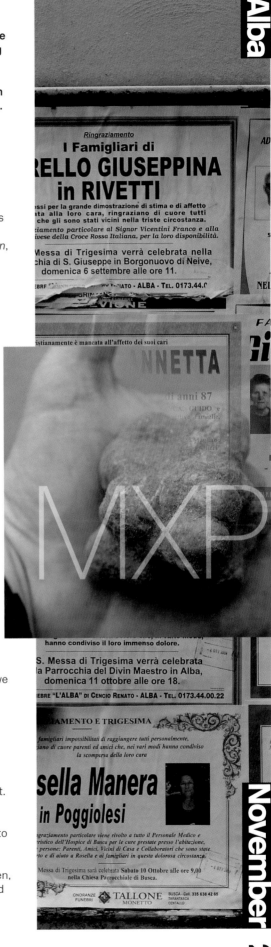

After lunch we were blindfolded and were hurried into one of Eledio's own truffle forests (yes folks, he has his own truffle forests!) We walked for about ten minutes and then Eledio's little dog ran, stopped dead, and started to dig – Big Nose was his name.

When we had gathered a handful of nice big white truffles we went back and were greeted by Eledio's lovely wife and daughter, who were making ravioli with basil'ed ricotta, tortellini with spinach, and bubbling gently, the local speciality bagna cauda made with their own olive oil flavoured with anchovies and garlic, in which you dip sliced pimentos, fennel, carrot and anything else you may have sticking out of your vegetable garden. We washed down the delight with a glass or two of the good man's wonderful wine.

If the truth be told, this is Eledio's daughter's recipe for bagna cauda, with my little squeeze of fresh chilli, I do hope she approves .

200 ml olive oil
4 garlic cloves, crushed
8 anchovy fillets in olive oil
¼ red chilli
The season's very best and freshest vegetables for example pimentos, fennel, green beans, cabbage, small carrots, celery, parsnips everything washed, some of them peeled and cut into strips.

Warm the olive oil in a heavy-based saucepan over very low heat, add garlic, anchovies and chilli. It should only be warmed and must not boil! It is important that the anchovies are completely melted before serving.

... imagine bagna cauda as a rather healthy version of the 70's phenomenon, fondue.

Eledio's bagna cauda

088

Cucina Italiano is a thing to behold, beautiful, simple – tasting a perfect saffron-seasoned *risotto alla Milanese*, or perhaps a *Minestrone d'autunno* with roasted ceps and dark Italian winter cabbage, Parmigiano, bread croutons and fresh truffle. Or a dish of rolled gnocchi over spinach and ricotta with warmed, garlic-infused butter. The Italian country kitchen is and always will be deliciously, oh so, *bellissimo*... if that indeed makes sense?

Polenta, the staple of the north, fried crisp with grilled lobster and lemons, or with slow braised neck of lamb with tomatoes, peppers and lots of garlic. In the regions of Lombardy, Trentino, Veneto and Friuli the inhabitants are known as *polentoni* (polenta eaters), a nickname from their fellow countrymen of the south. Up here a meal is rarely partaken, without the blessed polenta in one form or another. The ground corn was originally an every-day ingredient of the poor and the working class but now that polenta's homeland is one of the most expensive and sought-after regions in Italy, the traditions of polenta have thankfully stuck. Polenta is simply part of the soul of the people in this area.

Poor-man's polenta, primped...

FOR FOUR-SIX

600 ml milk
100 g polenta
1 stalk of fresh rosemary
80 g butter
50 g pecorino or Parmigiano, finely grated

VINAIGRETTE
50 ml white balsamic vinegar
150 ml extra virgin olive oil
1 shallot, finely chopped
1 clove garlic, finely chopped
Pecorino, finely diced
1 small or large fresh autumn truffle
Sea salt
Freshly squeezed lemon juice
A small handful of wild rocket, if possible

Bring the milk to a good simmer, infusing with the rosemary. Whisk in the polenta, stirring smooth with a wooden spoon, for five minutes. Remove from the heat and flavour with the butter, grated cheese, sea salt and lemon juice.

Mix together the white balsamic and olive oil. Add the shallots and garlic. Fold in diced pecorino and truffle just before serving. Season with a pinch of sea salt and a little lemon juice. The vinaigrette should be almost at room temperature when serving with the leaves of wild rocket.

Creamed polenta, vinaigrette, wild rocket

089

White truffle ice cream. Food of gods

090

This is not for children, folks. A white truffle is a jewel of nature, it should be respected and taken seriously – when considering the price! Once you have tasted this ice cream, there will be no way back; ice cream will never be the same again.

1 ½ LITRES OF ADULT INDULGENCE

600 ml condensed milk
400 ml cream
2 large tbsp honey
12 large egg yolks
1 small fresh white truffle

Bring the condensed milk, the cream and honey to just under the boil. Whisk the egg yolks until thick and creamy. Pour the hot cream over the yolks, whisking well, reduce the heat and stirring constantly, cook the cream until thick, coating the back of a spoon. Remove from the heat and grate the white truffle into the warm cream. Stir thoroughly and leave to cool. Run the cream through an ice-cream machine – storing in a freezer until needed.

I roll the ice cream here, in candied white chocolate, chopped dark and milk chocolate, toasted nuts and hazelnut nougatine.

Homage to Elvio the great, Alessandro, Fabio and John from Copenhagen's great *Era Ora*, who did me the honour of visiting my establishment a couple of years ago. This was the main course I made... they loved it and I was proud.

FOR MY FOUR PALS ITALIANO

500 g wild boar – neck or shoulder, cut into very large cubes
100 g pancetta in small cubes
Olive oil
4 shallots, finely sliced
4 cloves garlic, finely sliced
1 tsp finely chopped rosemary
2 glasses red wine
1 litre game stock
Salt and pepper
Mature balsamic vinegar
2 slices day old bread, cut or grated to small 'crumbs' toasted in olive oil
Truffle

PAPPARDELLE
1 kg durum flour '00'
1 tsp fine salt
10 large eggs
4 egg yolks
Butter

Start the day before by browning the meat well, together with the pancetta, in hot olive oil, in a large heavy-based saucepan. Add the sliced shallots, garlic and rosemary. Sautéing further, pour the wine over, reducing a little. Pour in the stock and leave to simmer over very gentle heat for two hours, until most tender. Turn off the heat, cool and leave the ragout to marinate, refrigerated overnight. For the pasta, knead the flour thoroughly with a little salt and the eggs, not forgetting the four extra yolks. When the pasta is smooth and elastic, film and rest in the fridge for a minimum of two hours.

On the day, gently warm the rich ragout through, simmer slowly over gentle heat. In the meantime roll out the pasta to the amount you need using a pasta machine if possible or a rolling pin like'a'mama. Cut with a knife, the more handmade, home created the better. Rest the pasta and then boil al dente in plenty of salted water, drain almost all of the water away and shake, enrich with the butter.

Season the ragout with balsamic, salt and pepper. Arrange together with the pappardelle, dressed with toasted breadcrumbs and grated truffle.

Ragout of wild boar, pappardelle, toast & truffle

091

The duck eggs from Eledio's farm are enormous, beautiful, creamy, intense – delicious. With their golden-orange giant yolk, like the late autumn sun of Northern Italy, and with their glass-like, almost transparent shell. Here with Eledio's white truffles, smooth, cappuccino in colour, with a velvet-like surface, they are creamy white inside. The wonder that is, *tuber magnetism pico* has the most intense aroma, and tastes amazing; Eledio's tubers were exceptional.

In my humble opinion, all truffles, no matter what the type and season, should be eaten completely fresh. Grated over scrambled eggs or with hot, steaming new potatoes and cold butter. Together with fresh pasta, a little olive oil and sprinkled with sea salt. Grated over a humble risotto and with a bottle of brilliant Barbaresco.

FOR TWO TURTLE DOVES

50 g butter, plus a little extra for the bread
2 large fresh duck eggs, lightly whisked
50 ml beautiful organic double cream
Sea salt
A little freshly ground black pepper
White truffle
Sourdough bread for toast

Melt a cube of butter over gentle heat and pour in the lightly whisked eggs. Softly and gently scramble the eggs. Add the double cream and season with a little ground sea salt and pepper. Serve with slices of white truffle and hot buttered toast.

Scrambled duck eggs with white truffles

092

Hong Kong

Many a time have I visited fantastic Hong Kong. My first time was just after the Brits returned Hong Kong to the locals... How do you return a country to the people that have lived there since the dawn of dot? It's a good job I'm a chef, and not a politician.

I was invited to Hong Kong by my old friend Henry who owns a food import/export business, he's a bit of a Del Boy, but based over there. We were eating out in a giant but rather ramshackle restaurant which had become famous for its dishes using the local pigeons. They tasted wonderful – sweet, sour, spicy, sticky and salty all at the same time – everything was fine, until later that night. In those days it was the golden rule, rather than the exception, that Chinese chefs splashed the food with the third secret spice, also known as E621 or MSG flavour enhancer. If you're not used to it and consume too much of it, it has, to say the least, some unfortunate side effects. I woke up in the middle of the night drenched in cold sweat with eyes that were so swollen I could hardly see, I only just managed to key in the number for the reception. Trying to explain, I could only grumble; my throat was swollen and I seriously thought that my last hour had come... and in Hong Kong of all places! The receptionist sent up a local doctor to see me. He looked at me and asked if I had eaten anything I would not normally eat... 'Well, what do you think? I was in Hong Kong for f++k sake, they eat anything and everything in these parts, if it moves and has a pulse, it's dinner!'... I told him that I'd done my best to keep up with the Jones' – well the Wong's in this case. The young doctor laughed heartily when I succeeded in explaining *where* I had eaten. The rather old-school restaurant was apparently notorious for their use and love of the super-spice MSG. 'That is why it tastes so good', maintained the friendly doc. These days the use of MSG, luckily, is not as common as it was back then, but you still have to be careful with the alleyway restaurants and street-food diners.

Hong Kong though my friends, remains a blast and a foodie destination to be reckoned with...

Guest chef'ing in the hotels and clubs of Hong Kong was a huge challenge, especially to begin with, but gradually I got to know the local chefs' mentality and understood the working routines, after which everything was reasonably painless. Hong Kong's chefs are, as chefs are in general, a proud, hard working bunch, fiercely loyal and for the most, responsible. As requested, I had sent my recipes and photos of my dishes in advance so they could get an impression of me and my style of cooking. When I arrived everything had been made exactly to the letter, perfection to say the least, I only had to taste, adjust and smile.

But I remember especially one warm, if stifling evening. There had been a party in the club. Five hundred invited guests of two most wealthy Indian families – a wedding of epic proportions, a glorious opening scene from a big-hit Bollywood flick. When the food was finally eaten, we left the club, out into Hong Kong's rainy night, leaving Bollywood for a rain-soaked scene from *Blade Runner*. We took speeding taxis through the deserted streets and arrived after some time at a completely dark quarter of town, with one flickering neon sign on the facade of a darkened office block and warehouse. 'HOTPOT' I could see, flashing through my soaked spectacles. We squashed together into an industrial elevator, went up to the fifth or sixth floor, the doors opening to a gigantic open-planned room with air conditioning going full force. There must have been 400 or 500 people in all sitting around large tables with steaming pots in the middle. They were enjoying the age-old Hong Kong speciality of hot pot – a sort of family fondue Hong Kong-style; pork stock with lots herbs, chilli and ginger, in which you dip almost anything. The boiling stock was now and then topped up with a little boiling water, but as the night drew on, it became stronger and wonderfully intense.

As more and more ice-cold beers went down, the old borders between Blighty and Hong Kong became gradually more diffused.

King Hong Kong

FOR FOUR OR SIX, RAIN-SOAKED AND STARVING

2 litres stock made from well roasted pork bones and a chicken carcass
1 large piece fresh ginger, sliced
1 chilli, sliced in half
1 bunch fresh coriander
1 small bottle good quality soy sauce

GARNISHES
Prawns, large, small and dried
Fish sliced, for example eel, bass, firm monkfish, weaver, scallops and oysters
Sliced beef, pork and veal
Calf's liver, sweetbreads and heart, thinly sliced
Breast of a chicken, pigeon or duck
Noodles
Bok choi and pak choi
Spinach
Cabbage
Beans and peas
Fennel

Warm the stock and add the other ingredients. Place over a hot plate (in Hong Kong they use small induction plates) in the middle of the table, placing small bowls around, along with the plates of garnishes. Serve with a good soy sauce, chilli sauce and steamed rice. Hot Jasmine tea and lots of ice-cold Chinese beer... we actually, after flying all that way, drank Copenhagen's own Carlsberg that night.

The stock takes flavour from the items dipped in it and gradually, as the evening progresses it becomes more and more concentrated and dark. It is not unusual to finish off by drinking the last of the stock, it packs a good punch.

It will be extra festive if you buy a few cheap bowls from your local Chinese shop, chopsticks and small tiny nets for the more fragile garnishes. They are very cheap.

Kowloon hot pot

093

Wan-chai, Hong Kong's very own Soho. Bohemian, full of individualists, the darkened streets are lit by flickering neon. Full of life, the bars, clubs, and the discotheques certainly have something for everyone, and for every taste. Places where one can meet the ladies of the night – and the boys... now't being too weird or too colourful for Wan-chai.

Food is fantastic in Wan-chai. The streets are alive with intense and wild flavours, just like the locals you'll meet within the area. There are no visible supermarkets – real live street markets are vibrant, full of the area's local people shopping for their daily goods... an activity that would be warmly welcome within the world that I live in. The back-to-basics ideals in the West seem further and further away – markets for me, harbour the very essence of life, joy and simple gastronomic pleasures.

FOR FOUR OR SIX BOHEMIANS

3 kg beef short-ribs
Vegetable oil
4 onions, sliced
10 garlic cloves, sliced
3 red peppers, sliced
2 tbsp sliced ginger
2 split red chillies
1 tsp coriander seeds
1 tsp fennel seeds
1 large glass hoisin sauce
200 ml honey
1 litre chicken stock made from a roast chicken carcass

TO SERVE
Fresh coriander
Fresh ginger
Chilli

Sticky ribs Wan-chai style

094

Brown the ribs very well, in the hot vegetable oil. Add the sliced onions, garlic, peppers, ginger, chillies, coriander and fennel seeds, brown. Pour in hoisin sauce, honey and stock and leave to simmer on a very gentle heat for three hours. Leave the saucepan with all its contents to rest, marinate and infuse, refrigerated overnight.

The following day, heat up the saucepan gently. Simmer until it thickens and becomes sticky, intense in flavour and well lacquered in colour. Dress with coriander leaves, sliced ginger and chilli, before serving with steamed rice and bok choi, along ice-cold Chinese beers.

... I f++king love Hongkong.

Wok no.1 was our nickname for the aging chef who was stationed at the first wok-section of the wok-department in the kitchens of the wonderful Hong Kong Country Club. There were over a dozen wok-stations, lined up along the entire length of the kitchen, looking and sounding, when at full-throttle, like the engine room of the Starship Enterprise. Giant gas burners behave like rocket engines, firing up under the traditional iron woks, which become almost instantly white hot and ready for cooking in a matter of seconds – the extreme blasts of heat being adjusted with a kind of pedal, which is controlled by a kung-fu-like twist of the wok-chef's knee.

FOR ME, BRUCE LEE AND MY TWO HK PALS URS AND JEFF

400 g neck or shoulder of happy pork
2 egg whites, lightly whipped with a fork
Sea salt
½ tsp dried chilli flakes
1 tsp crushed coriander seeds
2 tbsp cornflour
500 ml vegetable oil for frying
2 large onions, coarsely cut
2 cloves garlic, sliced
1 tbsp chopped ginger
1 red pepper, sliced
1 green pepper, sliced
1 red chilli, sliced
1 handful shiitake mushrooms
100 ml rice wine vinegar
50 ml light soy sauce
100 g sugar
Fresh coriander

Dip the pork strips in the egg whites, and season well with the sea salt, chilli and crushed coriander seeds. Cover and set aside for 20 minutes. Add the cornflour and mix in well. Heat a wok or a deep wide saucepan with the oil and fry the pork to golden brown and most crisp. Cook the meat a little at a time in order for the temperature of the oil to remain high, otherwise the meat will be boiled and not fried. Lift the pork and drain well on kitchen towel, keeping warm.

Fry the onions quickly with the garlic, ginger, peppers, chilli and shiitake mushrooms in a splash of super-hot oil. Add the vinegar, soy and sugar and leave to boil fiercely for two minutes. Season to taste with sea salt, and thicken the sauce with a touch of cornflour if needed.

Warm the crisp pork quickly through the hot sauce, dress with fresh coriander and serve with steamed rice.

Sweet & sour pork
by Mr. Wok no. 1

095

Hidden in the mountains, one and a half hour's drive to the north-west of Barcelona's airport, is the most charming medieval village, Vilanova de Meià.

The Catalans love to party, and every year in early November the residents of Vilanova de Meià celebrate *Fira de la Perdiu*, the festival of the partridge. 10,000 people converge upon the village, which normally houses only a couple of hundred within the aged city walls. Eating, drinking and making-most-merry... and not forgetting their beloved birds, preened and plucked, trimmed and tuckered, the wicker-caged delights are proudly showed in various categories, winning prizes as the year's best and finest young partridge.

For a good few years now, I've been down at the festival with a small group of chefs named *Arrèlia*. A few Novembers back we started to do small demonstrations for other chefs, the most delightful locals, festival participants and other gastronomically graced good people. This was followed by wine tastings, a culinary forum and a seminar with the local branch of the Slow Food movement. Afterwards we cooked a giant dinner on the stage of the village's old disused theatre, offering new interpretations of Catalan classics. *Pan con tomate* (bread with tomato, olive oil and ham). Sergi and Mads whisked up a wonderful *bacalao* (salted cod) with parmentière potatoes, followed afterwards by my braised rice and partridge, local mushrooms and herbs from the surrounding mountains. Cake was baked by Barcelona's own master-dessert-alchemist, Christian Escriba. Not a bad meal for the one hundred-or-so demanding guests, when you consider that everything was knocked together in a ramshackle, pre-Franco forefather's village hall, with only one gas burner, dating from before the First World War.

... yet another lesson in the art of simple cooking.

In love with Vilanova

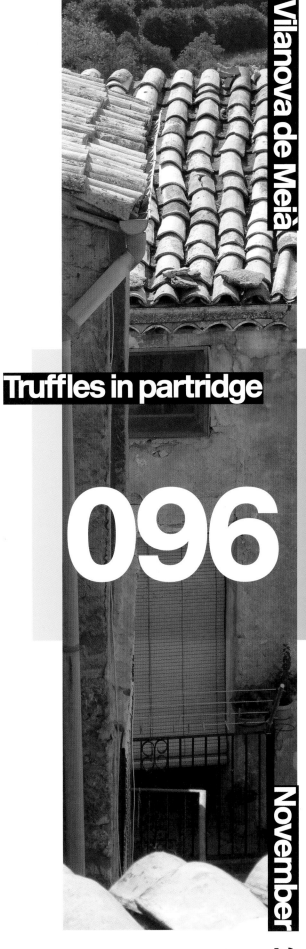

During this particular weekend, the town's longest street is full of market traders and folk offering local produce, from fantastic sheep and goat's milk cheese matured in rosemary needles, to mountain honeys with thyme and sage; the pine nut nougatine is immense. Spiced sausages, salted hams, cakes and the most wonderful flatbreads sprinkled with the zest of oranges and lemons, and glazed with sugar. Local moonshine spirits, red wine and bubblingly-brilliant homemade cava. Vegetables are brought in from the neighbouring villages, and it is during this weekend that the truffle season starts.

Sergi is one of my absolute best friends. His family have lived in the village of Vilanova de Meià for many generations, and he and his wife Sandra haven't taken long ensuring the next generation!

This recipe is from Vilanova's local café with a little Sergi-twist. Sergi is a truffle master and one of the most recent dishes I have had from his kitchen was a small salted, poached pork cheek glazed in a sauce seasoned with dark chocolate, and covered with just as many thick truffle slices, as the cheek was thick… f-a-b-u-l-o-u-s! His most masterly trick with the partridge is to place a small pungent, fresh truffle inside each plucked, prepared bird, leaving them in the fridge to absorb the flavours overnight. The meat of the bird soaks up the wonderful aroma from the fresh truffle, tasting amazing when slowly cooked the following day. The partridges are browned in olive oil with a little local salted ham and then braised slowly for a couple of hours with still more olive oil, a good slug of sherry vinegar, lots of onions and a small sprig of rosemary and thyme.

This technique could easily be used with guinea fowl, pheasants or indeed poussin. Partridge due to its very brief season, can often be difficult to get hold of.

FOR ME, SERGI AND HIS GRANDFOLKS

4 partridges
4 small fresh truffles
100 g salted, air dried ham or 75 g smoked bacon
100 ml sherry vinegar
4 onions, finely sliced
Olive oil, 200 ml in total
2 sprigs of rosemary
2 sprigs of thyme
Sea salt and freshly ground black pepper

Pluck and prepare the partridges and place a truffle in each bird, seasoning well. Cover with film and leave in the fridge overnight.

Heat a saucepan with two tablespoons of olive oil and brown the partridges with the ham or smoked bacon. Pour over the rest of the olive oil and the sherry vinegar, adding the sliced onions, rosemary and thyme. Season well with a little sea salt and pepper. Put a lid on and braise the partridges at a very, very low heat (approx. 125°C) for a couple of hours until tender with the meat melting from the bone. The birds should be turned and basted whenever possible.

Serve the tender partridges with the onions and the cooking fats. Brilliant bread and a small salad, possibly pureed potatoes too, seasoned with a little olive oil.

Truffles in partridge

096

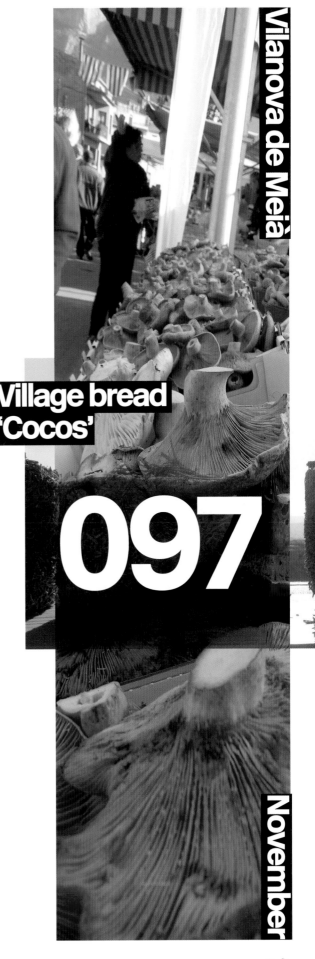

Rays of autumn light cascade over the mountains that surround Vilanova. Sergi's favourite baker is ten minutes from the town. We take an early morning drive and stop, as we always do at the humble little shop. There's a wonderful aroma wafting from the shop-door, so early in the morning, everything is clear and crisp, even the half-warm coffee in our paper cups seems to taste a little better. Adorning the window, the cocos glisten in the morning sun, glazed with sugar, honey and tiny pine kernels. They're baked in several versions; for the mornings with honey and dried fruits or maybe the sugared version with pine kernels. For lunch anything seems to go, from sardines with peppers and aubergines, chilli, spiced sausages and garlic to braised pork and button onions, garlic cloves and wild mushrooms, to small squid with wild oregano. I have also messed around with dessert versions to great success, bananas and chocolate, orange and pepper, pineapple and ginger... be free with your cocos amigos!

BASIC DOUGH FOR COCOS

50 ml olive oil
500 g plain white flour
10 g yeast
250 ml warm water
10 g sea salt – 5 g if you are doing the sweet version

Place all of the ingredients into a bowl and run it in the food processor for five minutes without salt. Then add the salt and run for another minute. Leave the dough to rest for a few hours, refrigerated.

Roll the cold dough into two long strips, about 2 mm thick. A pasta machine is perfect for this. Brush the dough with olive oil and top with the various ingredients.

Bake the cocos, crisp, in a hot oven at 225°C/gas 7 for about 10 minutes.

Village bread 'Cocos'

097

Yes, it takes three days, but it is undeniably worth waiting for! The earthy notes of the truffle with the sweet soft beef cheeks play delightfully well with the vanilla-perfumed potatoes.

FOR SIX

DAY ONE
6 large trimmed beef cheeks, each around 200 g
6 large sprigs of thyme, and 3 of rosemary
1 handful sea salt

DAY TWO
1 litre duck fat
4 onions, sliced
8 cloves garlic, crushed
Olive oil
2 large glasses red wine
1 litre beef or veal stock made from well roasted bones, dark and concentrated
Sea salt and pepper
Sherry vinegar
1 large fresh truffle

VANILLA POTATOES
1 kg winter potatoes, peeled
250 ml concentrated chicken stock
200 g butter (at room temperature)
Seeds of 1 vanilla pod
Sea salt

On day one place the trimmed beef cheeks into a sealable container, sea salt well and refrigerate overnight with the thyme and rosemary.

On day two rinse the cheeks lightly, and then place them into the warm duck fat, together with the herbs, and leave to simmer most gently for three hours until meltingly tender.

In another saucepan sauté onions and garlic in olive oil until they have coloured a little. Add the wine and let it boil, reducing by about half. Add the stock and reduce slowly until it has a thick, rich and sticky consistency. Season with sherry vinegar, sea salt and freshly ground black pepper.

Carefully remove the beef cheeks from the duck fat, being gentle so they do not fall apart, and leave them to drain a little. Place the cheeks into the slowly simmering sauce for about 30 minutes with half of the chopped truffle. Remove the saucepan from the heat, cool and leave refrigerated for the flavours to infuse until the following day.

On day three boil the potatoes until tender in well salted water. Mash the potatoes or blend them. Warm the stock and add it to the potatoes with the butter at room temperature. Season the potatoes well and flavour with the vanilla seeds.

Warm the cheeks thoroughly in the sauce, and serve in deep plates with the warm potato puree, grating the last of the truffle over just before serving.

Three-day beef cheeks in truffle with vanilla potatoes

098

Ramona's Paella

099

Ramona's paella from the local *Casal Municipal 'el café del Sindicat'* in Vilanova is fantastic. Artistically thrown together, rustic and superb, prepared in their most microscopic of café kitchens. A little chicken, a few sausages – shellfish, fish, greens. Real food by real folk.

FOR FOUR HUNGRY VILANOVIANS

Olive oil
4 shallots, sliced
4 cloves garlic, crushed
1 red, 1 green and 1 yellow pepper, coarsely cut
1 fennel, sliced – save the top for later
1 red chilli, split
200 g Spanish paella rice
500 ml shellfish – or fish stock
500 ml chicken stock
200 g spicy chorizo, coarsely cut
200 g chicken thigh, boned, skinned and cut into strips
500 g cockles and mussels, well washed of sand
8 large prawns – *or as many as you fancy*
Sea salt and freshly ground black pepper
A handful freshly chopped parsley

In a wide thick-bottomed pan, colour the sliced shallots with garlic in plenty of hot olive oil, together with the peppers, sliced fennel and split chilli. Add the rice after a couple of minutes. Leave to sauté a little before the heated stocks are added, together with chorizo and chicken. Leave the rice to simmer gently until it is almost tender, about 25 minutes. Continue to adjust the rice with a little water or more stock, if the pan begins to dry out.

Fold the mussels into the rice and season with salt and pepper. Arrange the large prawns on top and bake the paella in the pan, in the oven at 180°C/gas 4 for about ten minutes.

Let the paella rest a little before serving, dressed well with chopped parsley and fennel tops, drizzle with olive oil and serve with lemon and lots of bread.

Wild mushrooms on sourdough toast

100

We cooked the next dish at another party in the village when we were wild mushroom hunting. It was no easy feat but again 100 hungry partridge festival revelers, stamped their feet and chinked their glasses with typically warm Calatan enthusiasim. The quantities can be adjusted as required.

... the largest recipe in the book with no doubt the shortest text. Please adjust the quantities for your own little gathering.

I USED
A great deal of lovely local olive oil
About 15 kg of their wild forest mushrooms
50 finely sliced large shallots
50 crushed garlic cloves
Lots and lots of chopped mountain thyme and rosemary
A huge stack of sourdough toast from Sergi's local baker
Sea salt and freshly ground black pepper

In a big, big pot, we coloured the prepared mushrooms in shades of brown, golden and deep black. Sliced shallots were thrown in, with lots of crushed garlic. The sea of hot golden olive oil bubbled for a good twenty minutes, caramelising the pot's goodies, and we seasoned the mushrooms well with almost a whole bag of sea salt and two sore arms of ground black pepper. Cut the sourdough bread into thick slices and brush with olive oil, then grill. Arrange the mushrooms on the bread, sprinkle with thyme and rosemary and wash down with lots of local red wine.

Christmas at Cunninghams

I love Christmas and everything that goes with it... from the thick creamy eggnog with a dash of spirit to cheesy 80's American Christmas movies, German Christmas muzac programmes, cooked *klejner* (traditional Danish Christmas doughnuts boiled in rendered pork fat) and far too much roast duck, red cabbage and honeyed potatoes. At the restaurant Christmas begins in November, company Christmas lunches, Christmas menus, winter vegetables lifted with a touch of Yuletide spice. So much delicious food, so much wonderful wine and so many smiling faces. But the only thing I can think of is Christmas Day. My family, my kids, too much TV and my stuffed turkey.

On the 20th of December I usually fetch my mum from the airport, and dropping off her stuff we go with my boys to the closest forest of Christmas trees. Cutting down your own tree is the most normal tradition here in Denmark, but for us English, it's still quite new – completely fantastic. I grew up with a giant plastic tree in a thousand

On the house

different colours; glass baubles sprayed with glitter, metres of neon fairy lights and an inflatable Father Christmas hanging from the chimney. After a busy Christmas season a toned down, relaxed, natural Christmas is the only thing I ask for. Pine tree forests and new fallen snow. Wham's video for *Last Christmas*, realised.

On the 24th we have of course traditional roast duck, roast pork with honeyed potatoes, red cabbage, sour pickles and so-on, and so-on. *Riz à l'amande* (creamed vanilla rice pudding with cherry sauce), sweets and presents. And then the age-old jolly dance around the Christmas tree begins, a Christmas tradition that can't be broken... I think that you have to be born to this one, my two left feet come to life as soon as the first hymn beings to be sung.

The big celebrations in this land of Vikings and smoked bacon fall on the evening of the 24th. The following day, our children rise far too early. They know that their Danish gran has saved a present or two from the night before, for *Dad's Christmas Day*, as the day is called. We sit around the Christmas tree in our pyjamas and open our small presents, Bing and Elvis crooning in the background. We eat mince pies and drink tea. Maybe if I'm lucky I'll have a small glass of cream sherry, a wonderful if little old-fashioned English tradition. If we are very lucky my mum'll make a small bacon sandwich, with HP of course.

Not too long afterwards I'll adorn my apron and kitchen-mode kicks in, this time in true Floyd fashion, alongside a small bottle of red wine. At three o'clock I turn on BBC World, to watch my dear Queen Elizabeth's speech. An old royalist like me is very lucky to have all of two queens in my life! Well, in fact three, if I include my lovely wife.

A clink of glass and well wishes for the season are followed swiftly by our Christmas Lunch. A little plate of Scottish smoked salmon, lemon and brown bread, maybe a few small shrimps. Then roast turkey with my stuffing – pork farce, turkey trim, breadcrumbs, apricots, onion, parsley and sage, with this, boiled and roast vegetables of every shape and colour, small Brussels sprouts warmed with a few little buttered chestnuts, small plump pork sausages wrapped in a blanket of smoked bacon and a good strong gravy made from the juices of the roasting tin. After a much needed break on the sofa, I have my Christmas pudding and custard. Custard is heavenly! A warm velvet soft vanilla cream so thick that it clings to the pudding like real gravy clings to potatoes.

After the washing up and a good long walk along the beach my adored annual James Bond film calls. The coffee table is laid with clementines, oranges, mother-in-law's biscuits and the world's best sweets, Quality Street. We watch the film with half open eyes and the house is now quiet, my mum, mother-in-law and my wife are chatting over a cup of coffee, Valdemar, my youngest, is sleeping soundly and Christian, my eldest is playing with yet another new box of Lego. For the time being all is peaceful, all is quiet at the Cunninghams.

My Yuletide turkey with *all the trimmings*

1 fresh turkey of 4.5 kg

MY STUFFING
2 large handfuls breadcrumbs, fried in butter
250 g good pork mince
1 onion, finely chopped
1 small handful of coarsely chopped sage and 1 of parsley
1 small handful of chopped dried apricots
2 eggs
200ml milk
Butter or olive oil for brushing
Sea salt and freshly ground black pepper

Turn on the oven to 190°C/gas 5. Mix all of the ingredients for the stuffing, seasoning well. Push a little under the skin of the turkey, and the rest inside. Brush the turkey breast with olive oil or melted butter and season the turkey inside and outside with salt and pepper. Roast the turkey slowly for about 2½ hours (depending of the size) – basting regularly with the roasting juices.

Happy Christmas!

A remnant from the 1970's, a real family classic. This is a little different using the wonderful Danish langoustines from the island of Læsø, instead of prawns, and the smoked salmon somehow just belongs. I usually whip-up two kinds of cocktail sauce, a mild one that the children love and a slightly more spiced version, which I first had at the infamous Joe's Stone Crab restaurant in Miami.

Prawn cocktail anno 1969

FOR TEN PEOPLE

20 large fresh langoustines
10 slices of really good deep smoked salmon
5 baby gems, washed and dried
The seeds from 5 beef tomatoes
Cocktail sauce
5 lemons

Boil the langoustines in salted water for two minutes. Leave to cool a little and then peel them. Cut the salmon into strips. Serve the langoustines and the salmon arranged on the lettuce. Sprinkle the tomato seeds on top and place half a lemon on each plate. The cocktail sauce can either be served on the side in a bowl or you can pour it over the dish.

SAUCE MARIE-ROSE FOR THE LITTLE ONES
200 ml mayonnaise
4 tbsp ketchup
½ tsp cayenne
A little lemon juice

Mix and infuse for about one hour.

KEY WEST SPICED COCKTAIL SAUCE
200 ml mayonnaise
2 tbsp mustard
2 tbsp chilli sauce (it should be strong and not too sweet)
1 tsp grated ginger
½ tsp crushed garlic
1 spring onion, finely sliced
Finely chopped fresh coriander
A little lime juice
Sea salt

Mix and infuse for about one hour. The sauce is also brilliant with crab, lobster and even grilled oysters.

I am the only one in our house, who truly understands the magic that is Christmas pudding. The others have chocolate pudding, lemon pie or ice cream, fruit or Quality Street. So I usually end up sitting by myself, alone with my paper Christmas crown, enjoying my pudding in front of the TV. *Luv Christmas I do!*

Christmas pudding, adapted from the 1923 edition of Mrs Isabella Mary Beeton 1836-1865

FOR ONE LARGE (OR TWO SMALL) CHRISTMAS FIGGY PUDDINGS
75 g fresh figs, chopped
50 g sultanas
50 g dark raisins
50 g candied citrus peel
120 g ground almonds
75 g fresh breadcrumbs
75 g almonds, lightly toasted and chopped
50 g pine nuts
50 g Brazil nuts, chopped
75 g soft butter
Finely grated zest and juice of 1 orange
Finely grated zest and juice of 1 lemon
2 eggs, lightly whisked
½ tsp allspice
½ tsp ground ginger
½ tsp ground cinnamon
¼ tsp fine sea salt
75 g muscovado sugar
2 apples, grated
75 g honey
50 ml whisky
50 ml rum
50 ml brandy

Mix all the ingredients thoroughly and leave aside, covered overnight, either in the fridge or in a cool cellar. Then press the mixture into one large or two small thoroughly greased pudding basins.

Steam the basins in a large saucepan in water for three hours. The water should not cover the basins completely (the water must under no circumstances get inside the pudding) and they should be covered either with a lid or with foil.

Flambé the pudding in brandy and serve it with a blanket of warm custard, or indeed brandy butter.

When lunch is over and the sofa is calling... shortbread-based, chocolate-endowed coffee marshmallows!

SHORTBREADS FOR ABOUT 50 SMALL BISCUITS

450 g butter (at room temperature)
Seeds of 1 vanilla pod
Finely grated zest of half a lemon
150 g sugar
700 g plain white flour
30 g cornflour

Cream the butter well with the vanilla seeds, lemon zest and sugar. Sift in the two flours and quickly fold into the butter mixture. Form the dough into rolls with a diameter of about 4 cm. Wrap in film and place into the refrigerator to chill well for two hours.

Remove the dough from the fridge and cut it into slices each 2 mm thick. Place the slices on a baking tray lined with baking paper and bake for 20 minutes at 150°C/gas 2, not colouring too much.

COFFEE MIXTURE FOR 25 MARSHMALLOWS
200 g egg whites – please weigh the whites, it's much more
   accurate giving a better result
30 g sugar
100 g water
300 g sugar
150 g glucose
2 tsp very finely ground coffee

800 g dark chocolate
200 g cocoa butter

Whisk the egg whites with the 30 g sugar until stiff. Boil the water, 300 g sugar and glucose up to 117°C, measuring with a sugar thermometer. Whisk the warm syrup very slowly into the egg mixture, a little at a time ending with the finely ground coffee. Whisk the mixture thoroughly until cool.

Pipe the coffee meringue onto small shortbread bases, place them on a tray, into the freezer for 30 minutes. In the meantime melt the chocolate over a bain marie and mix in the cocoa butter. It should be around the 38°C mark when you are using it. Dip the marshmallows carefully into the melted chocolate butter, leave them to set and eat immediately.... they won't last long!

**Coffee
marshmallows**

Humble, heartfelt thanks

Santiago de Compostela
Paris
Korsør
Essex
Mauritius
Tokyo
Miami
Milan
Korsør
Barcelona
London
Cornwall
Sejerø
Dream Paradise
Gotland
Feddet
Denmark's west coast
Gisselfeld
Læsø
Bornholm
Scotland
New York
Alba

Line Thit Klein – photographer extraordinaire; an effortless pleasure of pure, immediate inspiration. I will never be able to explain to you the feelings and respect I have for your work – and Marie-Louise, photographic-assistant-most-exquisite.

Mia 'Panje' Rudolf; she took my scribbled notes, strange wordings and even weirder thoughts and lovingly made perfect sense of them.

Søren➔Grandmaster⬅Varming for being the royal that he indeed is. The Guvnor Sir, you are.

My untiring editor **Majbrit Hansen** – your patience is undying, unmeasurable, unsurpassed – most lucky I am.

Dearest Anne – so pleased, glad, proud I am. This is the start of something sweet.

My best'est buds **Kallen, Ashley and Alistair** – the lingual lords.

Without the likes of the great **Christian Mortensen and Daniel Walter Furmanek, Ragnar Erikisson and Jesper Tøtt**, Paul would not exist. I would be flipping burgers on a street corner – you guys have my ultimate, lifelong respect.

My mighty **Christian, my lill'Valde, my sweet Lene** – my love.

...and to you others – my family, my friends, my colleagues. This cooking lark, this restaurant business isn't the easiest of professions, it brings not the simplest equation to life's mysteriums – but love it I do, love you I do. My thanks, my love to each and every one of you delicious darlings – you know who you are.

**Your Paul
Copenhagen 2012**

This English language
edition published in
2012 by

Grub Street
4 Rainham Close
London SW11 6SS

food@grubstreet.co.uk
www.grubstreet.co.uk

Copyright this English
language translation
© Grub Street 2012

Danish edition ©
POLITIKENS FORLAG

Printed in Slovenia

ISBN 978-1-908117-22-9

Food portrait
photographer:
Line Thit Klein

World portraits:
Paul Cunningham

Graphic design:
Søren Varming

Danish editors:
Majbrit Hansen
And Mia Rudolf

Assistant layout:
Mischa Jemer

Translation:
Anne MarieTremlett

English edition
formatting and design:
Sarah Driver

English language
editor:
Anne Dolamore

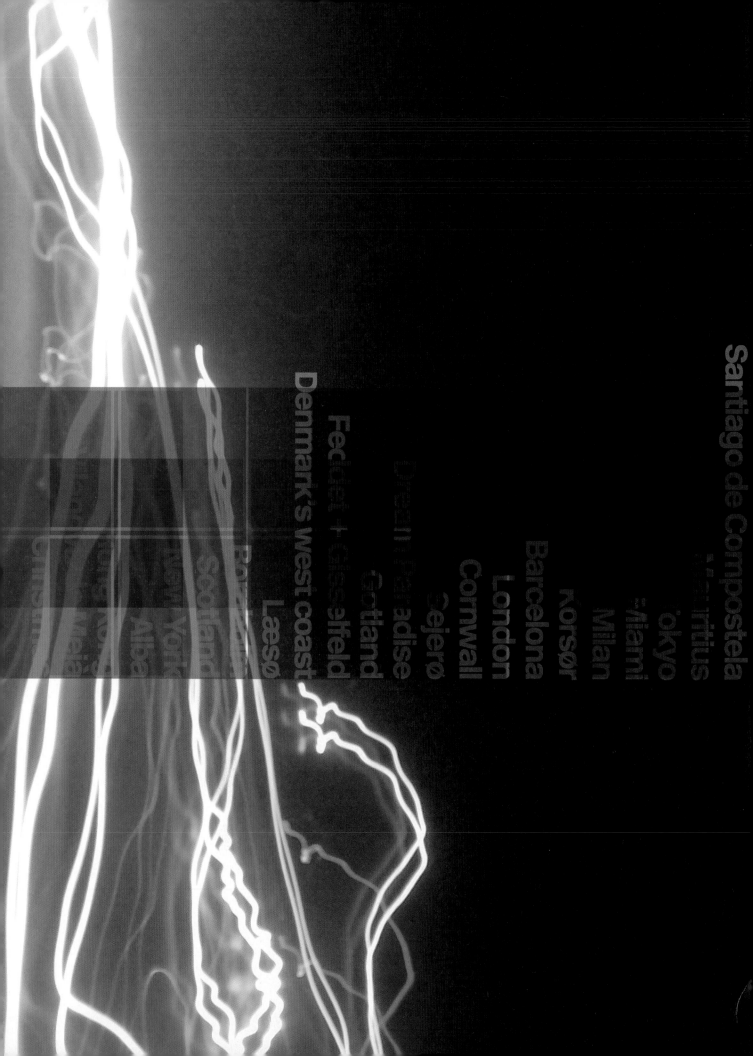

Santiago de Compostela
Mauritius
Tokyo
Miami
Milan
Korsør
Barcelona
London
Cornwall
Sejerø
Brazil Paradise
Gotland
Fedset + Gåsefeld
Denmark's west coast
Læsø
Bornholm
Scotland
New York
Alba

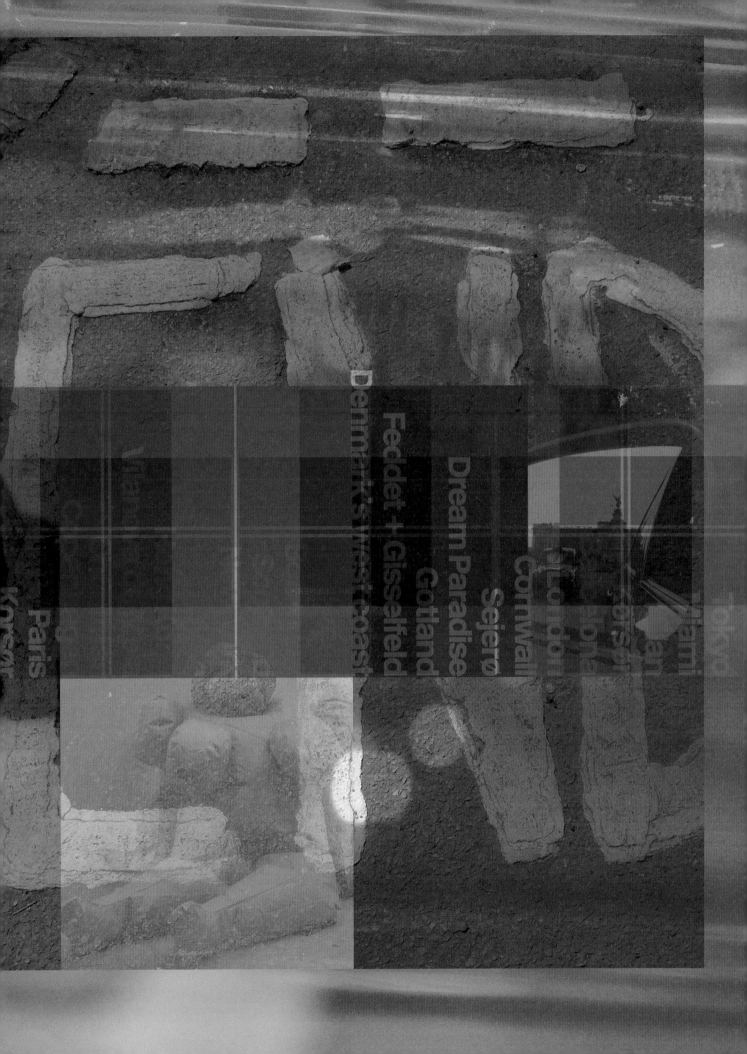

Korsør

Paris

Feddet + Gisselfeld

Denmark's west coast

Dream Paradise

Gotland

Sejerø

Cornwall

London

Tokyo